MW01709176

BEHIND THE VISOR

- MY LIFE IN WARTORN VIETNAM

Sister Sheila O'Toole RNDM

To a fantastic missionary and friend with all my love.

Special First Edition Copy
for
M. Agnes B

Sister Sheila
RNDM

First Edition August 2007

ISBN No. 978-0-473-12516-5

Typesetting and Design by Leeanne Phillips

Published and Printed in New Zealand by Print House Ltd

All photographs courtesy of Sheila O'Toole

This book is dedicated to the Sisters of Our Lady of the Missions without whom I would never have been in these situations, to the wonderful Stieng people whom I came to know and love and to the many wonderful supporters whose financial, logistic and material support made so much of this possible.

Sister Mary Laurence and Anh Hoa - learning from one another

Contents

Foreword

As a Vietnamese and a RNDM, I treasure Sheila's book, Behind the Visor, as it holds the memory of thirty years of the history of our country and of our province, a history of painful losses and heroic revival.

Furthermore, Behind the Visor illustrates very well the missionary charisma of our RNDM way of life, the sisters' courage, their willingness to risk all and their love for the poor and the marginalized.

Sheila's narrative awoke in me the memory of the valiant RNDMs from our other provinces who have played a special role in the life of our province.

I am grateful to Sheila for helping all of us to nurture our collective call to mission as RNDMs. Her story is a challenge to all of us.

Kim Phung, RNDM

Rome, May 2007

Author's Note

The following pages have been written to record my own experience and that of our Sisters during the terrible events that marked the conflict in South Vietnam during the invasion from the north, and led up to the fall of Saigon and the establishment of a Communist regime. The horrors and violence of those days and the sufferings of so many innocent civilians are very deeply embedded in my memory, and I still wonder at times how my RNDM companions and I survived our forced march through the jungle under the watchful eyes of North Vietnamese troops.*

As you read these pages recounting that experience, and the later desperate efforts to help ourselves and others to escape from the chaos in Saigon as the enemy closed in, it is my hope and strong desire that you will realise that the story is not so much an account about what we did ourselves, but it is more truly about the incredible love that God showed us as He journeyed step by step with us during those dark days. The simple message engraved in my own heart is that we can all count on this love and protection as we continue on our life journey towards eternity.

My prayer for each one of us is that we will never give up relying on this loving protection of our God and on His attentiveness to the prayers that are being offered for us by others. I truly believe that the prayers of our own Sisters around the world saved our lives and brought us through the ordeal. For this I will be forever thankful.

Special thanks to all who have encouraged me to write the following - too many to mention by name - and to all those who have spent time at the computer and offered suggestions:

John Kelly

Province Leadership Team, Aotearoa, New Zealand

Sister Patricia Hogan - RNDM

Sister Jane Kuklinski - RNDM

Sister Marie Gaudrey - Congregation of the Sisters of Mercy

Sister Mary Philippa - RNDM who spent some weeks with me bringing it all together.

Brian and Robyn Parkinson

* Religeuses de Notre Dame des Missions: Sisters of our Lady of the Missions

Nun Goes To Vietnam – With Circular Saw!

(Extract from Zealandia March 27th 1969)

Sister Mary Laurence holds her gift tape-recorder and two of the dolls that had been collected for Vietnamese children. Behind her are some of the cartons and boxes of goods with which the Sisters are trying to lift the spirits of the Vietnamese. Its simply written in the wooden crate containing Sister Laurence's circular saw. The scotch whisky box is not true to label. It simply indicates they have had to grab every available box to pack their consignment.

Everyone knows that women travellers carry enormous amounts of luggage. But Sister Mary Laurence O'Toole, headed for Vietnam, would beat them all for volume and unusual items of baggage.

Her bulkiest piece is a heavy wooden crate containing a circular saw and a full range of carpentry tools – hammers, saws, chisels, spanners, electric drill, electric sander, screwdriver, nails, etc.

These are not brand new pieces which Sister is going to hand over to the locals in Vietnam. They are much used items of personal equipment which will enable her to do a personal reconstruction in that war-torn country.

Standing trim and smiling in her religious habit, Sister Mary Laurence looks like many other Sisters of our Lady of the Missions, but her secret is that she is an accomplished carpenter and cabinet maker, who has left her mark on a number of convents in the Auckland Diocese. This all round ability was obviously a factor in her selection from local volunteers to do missionary work in Vietnam. She will join the famous Aucklander, Sister Mary Floride McCarthy at Thu Duc, who has worked in Vietnam for well over forty years, and was for many years the only New Zealand sister in that country. Sister Laurence left by air last Monday.

It was the Order's Provincial, Mother Mary Gerard, who revealed the sawdust in Sister Mary Laurence's past. She explained that Sister Mary Laurence is not only an artist of the circular saw, but a kind of general handywoman, who is adept at minor and electrical repairs, wields an effective spanner on motor-mowers, and tackles routine car maintenance jobs, such as cleaning the spark plugs.

With the co-operation of RNZAF Transport Command and the Army, plus assistance from NZ Embassy staff in Saigon, Sr. M. Laurence is able to present a small mission school at Thu Duc with items donated by the public.

PART 1

Republic of Vietnam (South Vietnam) 1955 - 1975

This diagram shows the approximate boundaries of the provinces during this period and is intended only as a guide.

Chapter 1

Young Missionary

In March 1969 I acquired a passport for the first time in my life. After being duly schooled as to its importance I felt complete in my preparation for my new venture.

I had spent some months searching for and devouring the scant material available on the culture of Vietnam. I had swotted up a little basic French, which I understood to be the official language there. (Until recently Vietnam had been a French colony - French Indo-China). Now I was setting out with some trepidation, a lot of hope, and little idea of what was really ahead of me in my new mission appointment. The Vietnam war was at its height too, but war was something totally removed from my experience; I wondered if it was all that the media made of it.

After a short stop-over in Melbourne with our Sisters I started the second leg of my trip, the flight to Saigon. Now what? I thought.

This long journey was my first experience of international flight - if it came to that, my first experience of flying at all, apart from being taken up in a bi-plane by a friend at the age of seven or eight.

This was the real thing! On board the big plane I read every notice - what to do in an emergency - how to put on the oxygen mask, where to find a floatation cushion, how to abandon my shoes and fling myself out of doomed aircraft. I did not fancy trying any of these measures when all we could see through the windows was white billowing clouds. I wanted no problems at all.

I placed the precious passport in the pocket of the seat in front of me, belted myself up firmly, sat tight and prayed for a safe landing. My prayers were answered and at last we came down uneventfully at Saigon airport.

I can't remember much of my first impressions. It was all a great buzzing confusion at the time - the excitement of the passengers getting their luggage out of the overheads, the general impatience to get out and away. I joined the bustle and followed the crowd into the terminal. There everybody started rummaging in handbags and pockets for - PASSPORTS! My heart stopped - crashed down to my boots - I saw mine still safely stowed in the pocket in the plane.

I rushed out of the terminal building. The plane was away over there! An empty luggage carrier was being driven past. Desperate, I ran out and stopped the driver, begging him to take me back to the plane. He kindly did so. How lucky I was that he could understand English! To my great relief the crew were still on board but my despair grew by the moment. No-one could find the lost passport. They even allowed me back into the plane to search for myself. Sure enough it was not where I'd put it. At last one of the crew informed me that it had been taken over to the terminal.

Back I went on the luggage carrier, wondering how and where to apply for lost property. Sick with worry I walked into the crowded hallway. Not far away an official was waving his arm high above all the heads, waving a small item - a small black item - a New Zealand passport - waving for its owner to come and claim it. Imagine my relief! Once that hurdle was overcome the rest seemed easy. Nothing would ever worry me again, I thought. Collecting my luggage, I was ready to step out into the unknown.

How pleased I was to see two Sisters, Gwen Mary of New Zealand and Marie Monique of France, waiting to welcome me as I trundled through into my new world.

Heat! What unimaginable heat! It seemed to rise up before me like a wall of fire as we stepped out of the building on to the street. I had barely registered this when the next shock hit me. A man was propped up against an outside pillar, covered in blood. No-one commented. No-one even glanced at him. No-one was doing anything for him or even noticing him. My first instinct was to stop and try to help but my two companions seemed quite uninterested.

Why don't they stop? Why don't they do something? I thought. They must have seen him or they must know something I don't! So I followed them blindly. (Over the years that followed I too grew accustomed to such sights, sometimes, and more often than not, faked by professional beggars playing on the goodness and generosity of tourists).

The drive out to our convent sixteen kilometres away at Thu Duc was hair-raising in the extreme for a Kiwi traveller - horns blaring, cars and bikes all vying for a place on the road, and no-one prepared to look out for anyone else in the world. I was convinced that no-one here knew or kept road rules. It was free-for-all and the survival of the fittest.

Rolls of barbed wire seemed to encircle every building we passed. People walked along the sides of the roads. There were no footpaths. Military personnel were conspicuous with guns always over their shoulders. Military vehicles, American and Vietnamese, roamed around the streets. (One day much later another Sister and I actually hitched a ride in an American Army tank because we had missed the last bus home from Saigon to Thu Duc). Everywhere there seemed to be military look-out points, particularly in the middle of bridges or at either end. Their job, they told me, was to ensure that the bridge was

not blown up from the river beneath. The Viet Cong, the Communist partisans, would place explosives on small bamboo rafts and float them downstream to explode and demolish important bridges. Dirt and rubbish were strewn anywhere and everywhere on the streets and chaos seemed to reign among the masses of people on the move. What a contrast to the orderly world I had left!

Indoors the convent was cool and clean and the Sisters gave me a great welcome. There were about twenty of them in the community but few who could speak a little English, apart from two Irish Sisters. There were other women too who helped out in the big and busy household. The establishment was much larger than I had expected. There was a boarding-school attached to the secondary school, kitchens for children and community, the Sisters' novitiate, and a house for aspirants to our congregation.

I was shown to my small room on the third floor. Sister explained carefully to me how to attach the four uprights to the bed-frame to hold up the necessary mosquito-net. I listened intently and thanked her but I am sure I could not have taken in half of what she was saying. One thing that did register, though, was the fact that water was precious. I was sharply called to order when someone heard me running water as I cleaned my teeth. One was never to let a tap run idle for any reason. Buckets of water had to be used to flush the toilets. There was no pull-chain or push-button flushing system here. By the end of that first day I was more than pleased to crawl in under the mosquito-net and try to sleep in the relentless heat.

It was Holy Week when I arrived. With the overpowering heat day and night, the Easter ceremonies all in a foreign language were not really conducive to attentiveness and devotion. Gradually it began to dawn on me where I was. I began to realise how much more difficult it is for missionaries to cope in situations complicated by lack of language and understanding. The smells, the food, the streets, the shops - how very strange, but in other ways, how exciting too!

The streets were full of stalls rather than shops and poverty was evident everywhere, the sheer mass of people trying to earn a pittance in the oddest ways, the hovels, the rags, the dirt! And the paradoxes too:- the people who could emerge spick-and-span, clad in spotless white, from huts in the filthy slums.

The first things that had to be attended to were the requirements of the Government in the form of papers and photos. A trip to the photographer's "studio" really was an experience. This establishment was a small hut on the side of the road with sacking across the doorway. Inside was a stool on which to sit (and smile when the urge took you) while the photographer clicked his camera at the right angle.

After a week or two everyone agreed that as soon as possible I must find a teacher and begin to learn the language. Necessity is a great teacher and I very quickly learned to ride a motorbike. Every day I rode the sixteen kilometres to Thi Nghe for lessons. I can't say that I learned much. Just trying to keep awake in the heat was well-nigh impossible.

There were other things too to keep me busy. After a while the Sisters asked me to take an English-language class in the secondary school, and when my circular saw and tools arrived (courtesy of the New Zealand Army) I set up a small workshop in a little shed in the grounds, hoping to start some woodwork projects in the near future.

One day towards the end of that year Sister Superior asked the assembled community if anyone could see her way clear to volunteer for work in the Phuoc Long area among the Montagnards or mountain-people, the tribal people recently driven from their jungle home by the warring armies. Like tribal peoples throughout Asia, these hill-dwelling peoples were often the target of discrimination by the majority group.

I considered the matter. It seemed to me that as a foreign national I would be much safer than any Vietnamese Sister in an area so politically unstable. Moreover, my craft and woodwork skills would be far more useful there than in the city. (It seems that Sister M. Thomas up in Phuoc Long had been praying for a helper with practical skills who could help the Montagnard men in particular. They were traditional hunters, fishermen and trappers, a seminomadic tribe now deprived of their normal livelihood).

My offer was gladly accepted and by Christmas I was packed up and ready to move.

Sr. M. Laurence, Sr M. Joan of Arc (N.Z.) and Sr. M. Monique waiting at the International Airport in Sunny Song Be

Phuoc Long

On Boxing Day, 1970, I set out from Bien Hoa military air base some distance from Saigon on a small six-seater Air America flight, accompanied by Sr. Gwen Mary. We landed on the main street of Phuoc Long, and came to a halt in front of the Province Chief's office. As soon as I set foot on the ground I knew it was the right place. It felt good and I felt right to be there.

Boarding the Air America flight at Song Be International Airport

The town, situated approximately fifteen miles from the Cambodian border along the Ho Chi Minh Trail, consisted mainly of a military outpost for army personnel and their families. Through the valley ran the beautiful Song Be river, often the only source of water for existence and for crops. The soil was deep red laterite, agriculturally some of the best, but in the monsoon season it became slippery red mud, whereas during the dry season it became fine talcum powder, covering everyone and everything with red dust.

Phuoc Long 'International Airport'. Sr. M. Joan inspects the interior of a helicopter

The community of Sisters consisted of Sister Mary Lea, who was Chinese born, Mary Thomas, English, Mary Christiane and Mary Angele, who were Vietnamese, and I made the fifth. A sleeping block consisting of five rooms, toilet and shower and a corridor had just been completed for the convent.

There was a school building at the bottom of the garden where Sisters Mary Christiane and Mary Angele taught the ethnic minority children from the many tribal villages situated on the outskirts of the town. Some of these children stayed with us as boarders because their villages were too distant for them to make the journey each day. Also housed in a small house at the end of the school was the family of Nhun, who worked in the garden and saw to all the odd jobs round about. He and his family were Stieng tribal people.

Sr. M. Lea with some of the children

Sister Mary Lea saw to the smooth running of the compound and house, and was Superior at that time. Sister Mary Thomas ran the dispensary, a makeshift room at the end of the kitchen-dining-room block. The dispensary was later rebuilt at the left of the main gate and this made things much easier for Sister as her health deteriorated.

I looked around to see where my work would lie.

The Workshop

Making bricks in the relentless heat with Sang, Toi and another young man from the village

Soon after my arrival I too could see that employment of the villagers was one of the immediate needs. It was to help the Stieng people that we opened a workshop in 1970, to give an opportunity to the men to earn a modest living. Many of them, especially the men who had been in battle, had lost limbs or sight. So there was not a great deal of work that they could be involved in and no one would employ them. Having some carpentry skills myself, plus tools, we felt that the best thing to do was to provide work in the form of furniture manufacturing. But where would we commence? The best place, we decided, was at the beginning, by erecting a workshop.

So we set about making homemade bricks with a mixture of laterite soil, some cement and plenty of elbow grease. We pressed the ingredients together in a hand press, after which the outcome - one brick - was laid in the sun to dry out. The first step must have taken us a few months to complete, with a group of the first workers who were with us to the end. I can't remember ever counting them but we must have made at least about 5,000 bricks in all, to do the walls from ground level up to roof height.

Cement for the project was donated by the Province Chief, while Sister M. Lea arranged for the sand and water needed. We chose a site just inside the front gate of the compound, on the right. As the structure began to take shape, the American servicemen situated in "Firebase Buttons" began to take an interest and to lend a hand, especially in the building of the roof. One evening, just as the men were preparing to leave for their villages, a gale force wind came

The workshop completed

Opening Day - Vietnamese Soldiers on duty

American and Vietnamese Officials

Tho founding staff

Thang, one of our best carvers at Phuoc Long

Some of the men at work

Sorting the rattan in lengths

Amputee at work

A suite covered with brightly coloured hand woven Montagnard materials

Loading up the furniture

Than engrossed in making a traditional fishing basket.

up and threatened to blow down all the scaffolding and framework. I rushed back and like Samson, but without his strength, tried to hold an upright in position. When the men saw me they rushed in too, and together we saved the day. Once the roof was on and the walls completed, we borrowed a concrete mixer from CORDS, (US Civil Operations and Revolutionary Development Support), and proceeded to lay a thick cement floor, much thicker than anything the local Vietnamese would have done, who could only see "colossal waste"! A half inch covering of cement was about their maximum. This two inch floor was still there thirty-four years later, in what remains of the workshop. We were grateful for all the encouragement and support we received from so many of the town community.

For our factory supplies we turned to the jungle. Rattan grew wild out in the jungles surrounding the town, so we felt that if we could use the local materials this would give more village people work, in collecting it for us - dangerous work, because of the Viet Cong, South Vietnamese who supported the North Vietnamese Communist military, and their mines. Encouraging the people to help out like this was not difficult as they would do anything if it brought in a little money. It has to be remembered that those who started work with me had never in their lives seen anything we would label as 'furniture', so the CORDS compound gave us on loan a Filipino man to assist us in the first stages of drying, moulding and constructing the first chairs and tables. The tribal men, being natural carvers, took to it like ducks to water, and the aid of a heavy rattan splitter sent up from Saigon found us turning out tables, chairs, and cots at an amazing pace and, above all, providing weekly wages for those employed.

The workshop bustling with activity

Some of the men in their native dress

A Montagnard with his bow and arrows

I soon began to pick up their language from working with them all day, and became not just the employer but a friend to their families and villages, which I visited as often as possible by push bike. Though this had not been the original plan, the workshop became an opportunity for the handicapped - mostly war injured - to have work and to earn a living for themselves and their families.

Most of the able-bodied men had been conscripted into the South Vietnamese Army, so there were few without handicaps to work with us.

Woy came in on his bicycle one day and asked if he could come and work with us. He was only sixteen at the time, but already had an artificial leg because of a mine he had stood on in the jungle. He was a lovely boy and soon learned from the men how to mould the rattan and weave the chairs.

Cay and his little girl with Monty

Cay was blind. He told me he had not been born blind, but had gone blind as an adult, and did not know why. His little seven-year-old girl would lead him in to work each morning from the village, and he would sit in his favourite spot all day, finishing off the strips of rattan with his

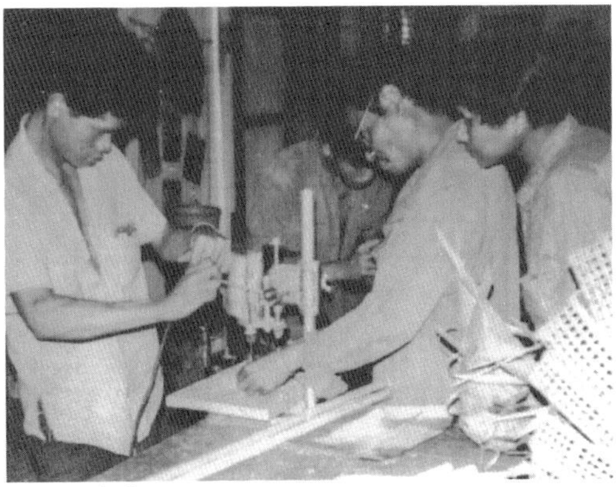

The workshop

A Trade Fair in Saigon - setting up our stall

knife, after they came from the machine. The work he did in finishing the material was perfect. While he worked, his little girl took part in the classes in our school until it was time to guide Cay home again. Monty, our little pet monkey, had a special affection for Cay, and vice versa - more about that later.

An outing with the men and Buttons, the dog

Visiting the villages to distribute medicine necessitated frequent trips after work

A leper patient in one of the villages

Assessing the needs of a family

The Stieng Tribe
Sister Mary Thomas, 1964

Meeting Sister Mary Thomas a seasoned missionary

The Stieng at that time had been brought into the town from the jungles by the Americans for their own safety and to save them being used by the North Vietnamese. The origin of these Highland Tribes of Vietnam, or Montagnards, is obscured in history. It is assumed that they were the original inhabitants of the country, and were driven into the high plateau by successive invasions. In 1964 it was estimated that there were 23,000 Stieng in Vietnam and 40,000 in Cambodia but war, malnutrition and disease have since reduced that number considerably.

The Cambodian Stiengs had had more educational opportunities; consequently, they were considered to be more advanced than their less fortunate brothers in Phuoc Long, Vietnam. The language spoken by the Stiengs, in no way resembling Vietnamese, is derived from two basic language stocks i.e. Mon-Khemer and Malayo-Polynesian.

Fear of Evil Spirits

The religion of the Highlanders is confused. They do believe vaguely in a supreme being but have no priests, places of worship or religious ceremonies. They have one thing in common with peoples of many other non-Christian religions - the Stiengs have an obsessional fear of evil spirits. These have to be appeased at any cost, even if it means the death or banishment of a dear one. This fear is also seen in their attitude to the sick. A doctor may be consulted; a patient may spend much time in hospital, but the sorcerer or sorceress has still to be called in, to perform his/her magical rite and so appease the god who is causing the illness.

Dignified and Courteous

Yet the Stiengs, who have no revealed religion, have many natural virtues in the practice of which they would put many a Christian to shame. They have a dignity all of their own, are very courteous and reserved and are very pleasant companions with whom to work. The Stiengs could be said to make their living by mixed farming. They cultivate their little rice fields by the slash-and-burn method; they hunt with bows and arrows and they fish in the Daac Glung river. They also grow the cotton from which their clothes are made. The latter are simple; skirts for the women, loin cloths for the men. Originally, the cloth from which these clothes were made had very intricate designs and often one skirt took two months to make. The dyes used were procured from vegetables. Such intricate work is no longer done; today the Stieng women prefer to weave a more simple type of cloth, even if it does mean less money.

The Stieng house is devoid of embellishments. It has just the bare necessities of life, a hearth, a bamboo platform on which they live and sleep, and a few baskets containing their earthly possessions, which are always packed in a state of readiness to move on to the next suitable site, when the fertility of their rice fields is exhausted.

Because of the invasion of the forest about 1957 by the Viet Cong, thousands of Stieng sought refuge, and still do, in settlements on the outskirts of the town of Phuoc Long.

As each new band of refugees arrives, they are given Government help in the form of rice, only for the first six months, after which they are expected to be self supporting.

For these people, used to a rural society many centuries behind our modern civilization, this change proves very hard. They find it almost impossible to cope and many succumb to sickness and suicide.

Musical Instruments

The Stieng are very musical people and have a wide variety of musical instruments, most of which were made from bamboo – the most famous, the set of seven flutes, T'met; the Ding Duot, a string instrument that sounds very much like the guitar; the Komduot made from a gourd and six bamboo reeds and sounding like an organ; and the Gongs, played on all important occasions, when the Stieng drink great quantities of home-brewed rice wine.

An Uncertain Future

The future of these people is very uncertain, as it is for many others in Vietnam. They are a thousand years behind our modern world; they are still in the throes of ignorance and superstition and enslaved through fear of their cruel Gods. The hope of the missionaries is that one day they will accept the 'Good News' and be free to live the life God wants his children to live, and at death to look forward with Hope and Love to returning to their Father's House. For this intention, dear Readers, we ask your prayers.

Laying Of The Foundation Stone

(Sister Mary Thomas's account of the new Montagnard centre)

The laying of the Foundation Stone at the Montagnard Centre of Phuoc Long was the fulfilment of a long cherished dream of the Sisters in the late 1960's. In early September work began in real earnest when the mountaineer soldiers and villagers started fencing and clearing the land around Moi Van Man Street, the chosen site for the new centre. The Deputy Provincial Chief, (a mountaineer), erected a platform, with a parachute covering for the principal guests, while on either side shelters were provided for two hundred mountaineers and for their special friends.

By 10.00 a.m. on September 25th everything was ready for the great day. Bishop Mai arrived with the chief of the Province and a representative of the American Army. Among the other guests were the parish priests of the nearby villages, the chief Bo New Zealande of the Phuoc Long Buddhist Pagoda, doctors, officers of the American and Vietnamese Armies, members of the Development and Relief services and numerous kind friends. Speeches were made by the parish priests of Phuoc Long, the Provincial Chief of the Province, Bishop Mai and Sister Gwen Mary. The latter gave her speech in Vietnamese which was translated into Stieng. The most important event was the blessing and laying of the Foundation Stone which made a very favourable impression on all present.

Like the scene from the Gospel the mountaineers sat on the ground for a meal of meat, bread, sweets and the traditional jars of alcohol. The other guests retired to a nearby hall where they were served with suitable refreshments.

In his generosity the Bishop opened the Golden Book with a donation of five hundred thousand piasters. This money was put to good use for the benefit of the poor neglected people of the area. Sister M. Rose who had worked so hard to make the celebration a success publicly thanked all kind friends for their generous support, assuring them that it would not have been possible to start construction work without their wholehearted co-operation. She hoped that the good seed which had been sown would in time bring forth much fruit.

- Sister Mary Thomas

Jian was an able-bodied young man who by rights was in the army but when he tired of the fighting he would clear off and come in to work until those in charge caught up with him again. He was a born leader and very concerned about other people around him. He would tell me who would need special help in the village and would often bring the sick into our dispensary. I relied a lot on Jian, when he was there! Another young employee of ours was a naturally gifted carver, who could carve anything with a knife from hard teak. All he needed as a guide was a picture. His elephants were no trouble to him as he was so familiar with them.

Tol and Sang were two of the first men we employed to help me make bricks. On them I relied when it came to the business of buying the raw rattan. (Years later Sang lost his life the day before we left Phuoc Long, when his village was bombed by our own Vietnamese planes).

As time went on we saw an opportunity of helping more by setting up a little shop in front of the workshop where people could buy things at cost. I asked Be if he would run it for us and he agreed happily. Be had worked with the Sumner Institute of Linguistics (SIL) to put the Stieng language into writing; he was the only one of the men who could read. Parts of the Bible had been translated into Stieng and Be was a firm Christian. I did not know it at the time but he would not serve any of his customers until they had heard a little reading from the Word of God.

In all, we were sometimes employing up to thirty workers, honest and loyal to the last. American supplies which came our way, we gave out to the people as supplements to diet. Food at that time was scarce and the Montagnards were suffering the most. I requested rice from the Provincial Government coffers, and when I went to collect a few sacks of rice I was asked what I was going to do with it. I replied, "What does one usually do with rice?" Did they think I was supplying the enemy? I wondered.

At that time people were so hungry that they would eat almost anything. One day when I was visiting one of the villages I came across an older man crouched in front of his fire roasting a rat on a spit - all he had to eat that day probably. I didn't stay in case he offered me a bite!

While working daily with the men and visiting the villages I gradually came to know more about their culture and beliefs. I saw on some occasions their fear of the "bad spirits". To lessen this fear they turned to their traditional witch doctors - often an expensive process.

One evening we attended a ceremony when one of the children of Nhun, who lived in the compound, became ill. Sister Mary Thomas had prescribed medicine and had also encouraged the parents to take the child to the hospital, which they did, and when the doctor examined the child he recommended that they stay there for the night or longer if necessary. That evening they were all back home and when we asked why, we were informed that the witch doctor had been asked to come and perform the healing ritual. Sister Mary Thomas asked if we could come too and the family had no objection to our being present. The ceremony seemed to consist of the sacrifice of a chicken plus the sucking of the child all over to draw out the demons. It was not very entertaining, to say the least. The child then recovered due to the appeasement of the spirits rather than any medication from the hospital, which was given no credit at all.

On another occasion Sang came in to us one evening in a terrible state. The village apparently had accused him of being a *Khak*. That meant that he had the ability to wish harm on anyone he chose so that they could even die. Sang vehemently denied this but when he realized they were going to kill him he escaped and ran to us for protection. We managed to get him to the hospital where he stayed in safety that night. By the next day the whole thing had blown over.

Sometimes the men would tell me of their beliefs in certain rivers and trees which they revered.

Once the young daughter of another of my men died in the village and the other members of the same village asked for time off to attend the funeral. I asked the family if it would be appropriate for me to be present and they had no objection. I felt this was a great privilege as I accompanied them from the village where the funeral started. Only the men were allowed to accompany the body, carried on a home-made stretcher from the house to the burial site. The women stayed at home to prepare the food. We walked along the road for some distance until we trekked into a bushy clearing where a grave had been prepared. The ceremony commenced with branches of trees being waved inside the grave to dispel any evil spirits that might have been lurking there. This rite was accompanied by a solemn chanting. Once the body was placed in the grave the men busied themselves setting traps all around to catch the wild animals for the child's food. Other things were left on the grave, such as some of the child's possessions, and of course, water. This all took a long time and after all was finished we returned to the village for the meal prepared by the women.

A market in a small town provided us with basic Vietnamese food, which in the beginning took me a while to adjust to. The meat stalls were a special eye-opener, as every cut of meat was spread out on a trestle, without any cover, and thus was difficult to find under the barrage of flies all over it. No one seemed to mind, and after giving the meat a good wash before cooking, it surprisingly had little adverse effect on us. Thank God, there was always fresh fruit.

Our electricity came from large generators a little way down the road from our compound. They were a centre of activity each night, as the enemy tried to put all out of action. Machine guns were the music that lulled us to sleep and often we were left in the dark without power. Sister M. Lea had large concrete holding tanks built to supply the compound with enough water to help us through the months of the hot dry season before the monsoon rains came. We had a couple of forty-four gallon drums on a high stand, into which Nhun pumped water by hand, to give us a little comfort in our house. Invariably, this supply did not see us through the dry season and we had to rely on a water-truck bringing in water, pumped from the small lake close by. Nothing was ever tested for cleanliness. We were only thankful for water. As for me, I preferred not to take the risk of looking for any problems.

The Parish Church that we attended was situated next door to an army camp. This seemed to be the general practice, so that the military would be harder to pinpoint if their camp was in and around civilians. One Sunday morning at Mass we heard an explosion close by and the whole congregation fell on the floor and under the seats. The priest was giving a sermon at the time, and I can remember him crying out, "Don't be afraid!" Luckily, that time the church was not hit, but a shell landed next door in the military camp. Constant shelling on the town became a way of life to be contended with, and we used to thank God when we heard the whine of a shell, which meant it was going over us.

One evening, a shell hit some Stieng houses down by the Song Be river, and four or five people were killed. I went out to the village the following day, and found one family taking the soft partition iron off their roof to make coffins for the dead.

Our Animals

There was little or nothing in the way of entertainment, but we made the most of what we had, and enjoyed the antics of our animals. The compound already had a lovely dog called Bobby when I arrived, and he was such a faithful friend.

One Saturday I set out on my push bike to visit one of the villages a good distance away. It was a lovely day and I was enjoying the ride, not being aware at first that Bobby was following me. I encouraged him to go home, but to no avail, and I was not inclined to turn around and retrace our path. I just had to decrease my pace, so that he could keep up. By the time we reached the village Bobby was completely

Faithful Bobby

exhausted and tried to find a sheltered spot in the undergrowth. I found some water for him and left my bike close-by while I went on foot to visit the people I wanted to see in the village. When I returned to my bike to set out for home again in the mid-day heat, Bobby had made up his mind to stay put. No-one was going to make him run all that way back again. What to do? One bike, one dog and me! The only solution - I sat Bobby on the seat of the bike, with his front paws on the handlebars and pushed him all the way home. He did not complain, and I was the one who was exhausted when we arrived back. (This dog later journeyed through the jungle with us, when we were fleeing the village under attack, and reached Saigon safely.)

Buttons, named after the American fire base, was a little puppy given to me by a young American soldier who asked me if I would look after her for him. My heart went out to this poor boy as he struggled to say goodbye to the little pet he had grown to love. It turned out, as some of his mates told me, that he had grown up in an apartment in the States where he could never have a pet of his own. He had become so attached to Buttons that when he was transferred to Saigon he was torn between taking his puppy with him, or leaving her behind. I promised to look after her for him, and Buttons became my constant

The passenger service with Buttons aboard and Monty in my pocket.

Buttons

companion over the years and was with us to the end. She produced a couple of litters of beautiful pups.

One day a young Montagnard boy came to the workshop door with a baby monkey which he had rescued when its poor mother was shot for food. He was hopeful that we would buy it from him. I knew it probably would not survive in the village and being naturally a soft touch where animals were concerned I got one of the men to bargain for a fair price and Monty became another addition to the family. She was a great source of entertainment to all in and around the compound. The initial problem, of course, was where to keep her. We eventually built a walk-in cage for her, in front of the workshop, where she grew and thrived on the food and attention coming her way. She became extremely attached to me, as before her cage was built I would pop her into the pocket of the carpenter's apron I wore all day in the workshop. There she was perfectly content to stay or to go to sleep.

Monty, hoping for a drink of real Coca-Cola

A pangolin which burrowed to freedom overnight

As she grew, Monty soon found ways of getting out of her enclosure and joining us in the workshop, where she would annoy the men by running away with their hand tools, scaling up to the roof rafters and refusing to come down and return the stolen goods. This caper could hold up the works for some time. One day one of the men had a brainwave. He came over to me and went into a great act of giving me a good hiding. This worked like magic. Monty was down on my shoulder like a shot, making terrible faces and noises to ward off the "attackers", the stolen goods long forgotten. She recognised the men she liked when they came in the gate in the morning, and acted accordingly to friend or foe. Some of the men would tease her, by giving their lit-end cigarettes to her, but she was too shrewd for them, and would turn the cigarettes around and throw them away.

One of her favourite places was the Sisters' dining room, where there was usually a bowl of fruit from which she helped herself. She was especially attracted to our blind worker Cay, and she would often stay and keep him company.

Sometimes after work was finished and all the men had returned home, I would take the dogs and Monty for a walk down the hill to the river. She would sit on my foot with her arms around my leg and expect me to carry her down. Once there, she loved the water, and would play as long as I was in sight. Sometimes I would sneak away and hide and she would begin to call out in frustration, or try to hitch a ride on Button's back. She gave us many a laugh and we all loved her.

"Well done good and Faithful Servant": Sister M. Thomas R.I.P.

Sister Mary Thomas was a Londoner through and through, who had answered the call of the needs of Indo-China when she went to join our French and Vietnamese Sisters in Hanoi and assisted as a nurse for fifteen years. After the take-over of North Vietnam in 1954 she, with three foreign Sisters, was evacuated to England. On arrival she was found to have TB and was taken directly to the sanitorium where she received treatment until she was allowed to return to the convent. When she was well enough, she helped in the science laboratory of our large secondary school in Wealdstone, until after fifteen years absence she again answered the call to mission and returned to South Vietnam.

When I went up to Phuoc Long she was the only one in the community who could speak English so over the years we became good friends. She was completely devoted to the Stieng, and would be on call twenty four hours a day if needed. She was not strong in health herself and when she became very ill we Sisters were all anxious for her to get to Saigon where she could get better treatment and a doctor when needed. She reluctantly agreed to this and was flown down to a hospital in Saigon where she spent some weeks before being transferred to our convent in Thu Duc. I drove down to Saigon to see her. By that time she was desperate to return to Phuoc Long so we twisted the arm of our reluctant superior and left for home the following morning, though it was a long tiring trip for her.

At this stage the mission was working consistently, the school was functioning well, and there was a group of children who stayed with us for the school year as their villages were too far away for them to travel backwards and forwards.

Sister M. Thomas took up her work again with the sick as soon as she was able. The dispensary had been rebuilt near the gate. There Sister spent all her time tending to the sick who came regularly, sometimes with ailments and often just to collect anything she could give them. Though so ill herself she made herself available any time for the people she loved.

Dr Merritt Stark was a paediatrician who worked with the American section of CORDS. He made frequent visits to Phuoc Long and was extremely good to us. He was especially attentive to Sister M. Thomas while she was so ill. When she died he made a special trip up to be present at her funeral.

Sister M. Thomas' only desire was to stay where she was, and to be buried close to those she loved. In April 1973 she passed away. She was accompanied to her last resting-place by many people from the town and by Stieng from the villages, who walked in procession down to the river-side where she had asked to be buried. The men from the workshop formed a guard of honour at the graveside to honour their true missionary to the end. She is still there today keeping an eye over the Stieng and looking after the missions the Sisters still run in that part of the country.

Dr Stark at Sister Mary Thomas's funeral

Chapter 2

Travels With A Kiwi

Situated as we all were close to the Ho Chi Minh Trail, we could never be sure that the roads were safe to travel on, and before we had a vehicle we were completely isolated. At that time, if it was necessary to go down to Saigon we relied on the kindness of the army helicopters, which were flying in and out to the military base. They even transported some of our furniture to the Saigon markets. At other times I flew up and down over the jungle, sitting beside an open door of the aircraft.

While we were still without a vehicle, the American soldiers flew an old jeep they had recaptured in Cambodia back to their base in Phuoc Long and proceeded to repair it and make it road-worthy again. In the process they "borrowed" parts from other vehicles in the camp, including the commander's headlights. When they were satisfied it was ready for the road, they delivered it to our door plus a trailer. This vehicle was very handy for our work of driving into the jungle for the rattan, although we often had to ask our soldier friends to repair it.

In the first year or two our only mode of travel in and around the village was by push-bike. In 1970 the New Zealand schools run by our Sisters combined to raise funds for us to purchase a small Hilux Toyota pick-up. This made a great difference to the help we could provide to the villages. We were more than grateful to all those involved in this gift. We had a Kiwi painted on the door and many were the adventures we and Kiwi encountered on the unpredictable roads.

Phuoc Long To Saigon And Return

It had been ten months since the road to Saigon had been closed but once a 'cease fire' was announced we could see no reason for not making use of the road again, especially since the buses had started running each day. We had a suite of furniture ordered by an American at Bien Hoa which needed to be delivered. I decided to take two of the Montagnard boys with me to help me unload and also to give them an opportunity of seeing Saigon. It took us two days to load everything into Kiwi - furniture, bows, woven material and other Montagnard handicrafts which could be sold in Saigon without any difficulty, thus giving the poor Montagnards some little income on which to live.

On Tuesday 29th February at approximately 7.00 a.m. we set out on a trip which proved more than interesting and one we will not quickly forget. We had covered the first 33 kilometres when we had to wait at one of our outposts while the road was checked for mines, both ours and the enemy's, which took half an hour. While we waited we could hear monkeys screeching in the jungle all round us and we looked with envy at the lovely trees which would have been ideal for our carvers.

Eventually we were given the all-clear again and off we went, though not at what one would call break-neck speed. To call the road a road would be a gross exaggeration and to travel at 20 kilometres per hour was, we felt, reasonably good. We travelled for the first hour or so without mishap when quite suddenly we came face to face with the Communist flag flying gaily from a bamboo pole attached to a log in the centre of the road. I could feel Woy and Diem stiffen beside me. At the same time two men, one in civilian and one in army clothing, signalled us to stop. One, who appeared to be in charge, wore a lovely leather holster over his shoulder, a pistol at the ready. He looked us over and asked where we were going and what we had in the truck. The other fellow hovered in the background, ready for any emergency. The boys must have answered his questions to his satisfaction as we were told to go on. "Well," we thought, "if it is as easy as that, it must not be too bad."

We changed our tune at the next stop. I can't remember for how long we had travelled before we were stopped again, this time by about twenty soldiers armed with tommy-guns and other weapons, who crowded around the truck menacingly. We had the South Vietnamese flag on the car and I think that may have antagonised them. The flag was ripped off by one of the soldiers who wore the appropriate expression to suit the action, tearing up the flag into small pieces and dropping them without ceremony by the roadside.

The boys were ordered out of the truck, and their identity cards demanded, not too politely, I must say. They asked the boys if I was French, but the boys said no, I was English. (I must apologize to the English, but we had to stretch the truth a little here as it might have been unwise to say I was a New Zealander.) Thank goodness, the boys' cards and papers were in order. The communists insisted for some time that they were soldiers and I had

Diem and Woy at CRS Saigon

an awful fear that they were going to take our boys off with them or, worse still, shoot them on the spot. Some very fervent prayers went up to Heaven in those few minutes. Diem was shaking like a leaf. He had every reason to be terrified. Both boys had been wounded during attacks on their villages. Woy had lost a leg and Diem had suffered shoulder and intestinal injuries, and had been left with a permanent limp.

At last the enemy forces were convinced that our lads were not soldiers, but then came the demand to see everything in the truck! As I said before, it had taken us two days to load everything and I had visions of spending two days in the jungle or on the road re-loading. The boys told them we had only furniture to sell in Saigon, but this was not convincing enough. The canvas had to be undone and everything seen. In the process a small box of medicines I was taking to our dispensary in Thu Duc was discovered; we were ordered not to carry medicines on the road and not to have anything tied up so that it couldn't be seen. I wanted to ask by whose authority these orders were given but I felt that my knowledge of Vietnamese might be insufficient. Anyway they had almost ignored me till now. At long last they told us to go.

The boys literally fell into the truck beside me and we couldn't get away quickly enough. We were stopped three more times after this but not subjected to such close scrutiny, though they all wanted to see the boys' papers and contents of the car. It was extremely amusing to see the expression on some of their faces when we drove close enough for them to see it was not a Vietnamese at the wheel. Their jaws dropped and continued to drop and their eyes opened wider and wider. One chap seemed to be struck motionless for some minutes! After five stops we welcomed the sight of the South Vietnamese flag flying again and breathed a prayer of thanks to God for seeing us through so far.

We were stopped again, this time by our own military who acted so much like the enemy soldiers that in the end I asked them who they were! That broke the ice and we were told to go on. The road ahead was full of bomb craters and shell holes and the remains of destroyed houses stood on both sides of the road as we made our way through Binh Duong. Eventually we arrived at Bien Hoa at about 2.00 p.m. and sought out the recipient of the furniture. I was very embarrassed of the dirt, not only of the car and its contents, but also of the three of us, so covered with dust we might have been part of the dusty red road.

As I had quite a bit of business in Saigon I did not expect to be finished and ready for the return trip before Friday. When we arrived at Thu Duc we found that Sister Marie Monique, Provincial Superior, was still in Nha Trang and, with all due respect to Sister, I secretly hoped she would not return before Friday as I had a feeling that she would refuse us permission to return by road and that is exactly what did happen. Sister returned on Wednesday and I understood her feelings when she heard our story, though I did try to impress on her that it wasn't as bad as it sounded and even invited her to accompany us back to see for herself but Sister wasn't having any of that. She said we could leave 'Kiwi' at Thu Duc until we could get some guarantee that the road was safe and return by plane in the meantime.

I left Thu Duc early Thursday morning to try to comply with her wishes but it was easier said than done to find air transport to Phuoc Long, especially since there were no more Americans up there and Air America had ceased its regular flights. In trying to find a Vietnamese Military office I stopped by accident in the grounds of the International Commission of Control and Supervision (ICCS) Headquarters in Saigon. Surely this was not just a coincidence. Maybe they could help me. It was worth a try anyway. So I went in and asked to see a member of the ICCS. I was shown into a room of Polish Officers to whom I told my pathctic story. I did want to return to my mission, and could they give me some security on the road? The poor things had not been confronted with anything like this before and just wanted to drop me like a hot potato, but they did not quite know where to do so. At last one of them had a brainwave. He sent me to a Canadian whose job seemed to be directing everyone to the right places.

That officer was very kind: he suggested I go over to the ICCS Headquarters at Bien Hoa and put my case to Major Missen, a Canadian in charge of the area in which Phuoc Long is situated. I thanked him most sincerely and set out for Bien Hoa with a real ray of hope. The Colonel was out when I arrived but while I was explaining my predicament to members of his staff he returned. Being a member of the Commonwealth had never before meant so much to me as then, and I felt a strong bond between us, especially when they learnt my nationality. They could not have been kinder and the Colonel said he would do all to help though, as I knew, my request did not really come under their jurisdiction.

After some discussion they suggested that I visit the joint member of the Provisional Revolutionary Government (PRG) Commission in Bien Hoa and arranged a meeting for that evening at 7.30 p.m. My spirits were high at the prospect of being able to return by road and on the way to Thu Duc I tried to explain to the boys just what we were trying to do. Everyone was keenly interested to hear the result of the forthcoming meeting as to our knowledge, no civilian had ever approached the PRG. We duly arrived back at the ICCS Headquarters at 7.00 p.m. where I met Major Missen whom I was to accompany to the arranged meeting with the PRG. Diem and Woy stayed with Kiwi while the Major and I set out in the ICCS car looking very official, flying its significant Black and White flag.

The looks of astonishment on the faces of the guards when we entered the compound were really amusing. They had never before seen the Major arrive with a companion, and certainly not, as this time, with a 'Nun'. As we were a few minutes early we sorted out our facts together in the car before going in and decided it would be better for Major Missen to state my request as they were used to him speaking and would probably understand him better.

At 7.30 p.m. we were greeted by the North Vietnamese Communist representative who showed us into the conference room. After introductions we were given some Vietnamese tea during which the Major Missen very clearly put my case before them. I wanted to return to Phuoc Long by road, but my Superior was anxious for my safety and could they give any guarantee that all would be well? One acted as interpreter while the other jotted everything down in a notebook. We showed them on the map the route I had taken and the exact route I would take back, travelling approximately 160 kilometres, perhaps a little more. They asked to see my passport which luckily I had with me, and I sent up a good few prayers while Major Missen answered their questions. At length the senior of the two said he would put this to the Commander, which he proceeded to do. On his return he told us it would be perfectly all right for us to return to Phuoc Long, that their policy is not to interfere with people on the road and we would be safe enough as long as we carried no arms with us. That was all I wanted to know. I thanked them very much, thankful I had not to wait two or three days for an answer. I lost no time in leaving in case they thought of something that might delay things.

We drove back to ICCS where I picked up Kiwi and the boys and returned to Thu Duc. Before leaving I thanked Major Missen sincerely for his kindness, understanding and real help. I feel proud I have met and spoken with such fine men whose job was by no means easy. May God guide them! Before leaving I asked him for one more favour: would he write down on a piece of paper where we had been, the request we had submitted, and the outcome, so that I had real proof to show my supcrior? (I still havc thc piccc of notcpapcr and the message he wrote.)

At 6.30 a.m. next morning we left for Phuoc Long. It's always a nice feeling to be homeward bound. We made good time until I missed a turning and travelled some miles out of our way, only too easy when one must rely solely on memory as there are no such things as sign posts! After what seemed ages we eventually got back on the right road. It must have been about 11.00 a.m. when we met more of our 'friends'. They did stop us but were not nearly as aggressive as before, and I felt the message must have surely reached them. In fact we were asked to give a lift to two of them to the next post up the road and both piled in, packs, ammunition, guns and all. Perhaps I could have been had up for 'collaborating' with the enemy but we had no option.

We were stopped eight times in all on the return journey but apart from one fellow who couldn't find anything in our truck that suited him except two tins of drink and an empty sweet tin we were not bothered too much. How glad we always were to spot a South Vietnamese flag flying and to wave to our troops when we passed them. We had one last wait a few miles out from Phuoc Long while our troops investigated a suspected mine on the road. We finally reached home at 5.00 p.m., most grateful to Jesus and His Holy Mother for their ever watchful protection, and for the gift of good friends whom we met everywhere and who were always out to help us.

It was truly an eventful and most interesting trip and I resolved that if I ever did it again, I would see that I carried a spare South Vietnamese flag tucked away in hiding in case another was confiscated. There were other occasions like this as the following copy of a letter written to the Sisters shows.

Copy of a letter written to the Sisters in New Zealand

24 June 1974

Another trip which was the outcome of one of those split second decisions - all got underway so quickly that I hardly knew I was going until I found myself on the road. As I think I told you, we now have a new shop in Saigon, built especially for the ethnic minorities to display and have an outlet for their goods. Up till now we had sent no furniture down, one reason being that we wanted to make the load worthwhile and the other that the transport difficulties are still with us. However, last Saturday I decided that we had enough for a good load and went in search of a merchant who makes frequent trips to Saigon, to see if he would take it down for me. He agreed but - at a price!! A price so far exceeding our pocket that it would not even be worth our while! It was there and then that I decided to go myself, so I spent all day Sunday packing Kiwi to bursting point and was all set to leave Monday morning. I waited for the men to come in to work so I could tell them that I was going and to make sure they all knew what to go on with until I got back. Woy, one of the boys who accompanied me before, came with me and we set out at approx. 8 a.m. It was teeming with rain as only the monsoon can do, and not many who saw us leave expected our little truck to be able to weather the storms or the road but they don't know the endurance of our "little Kiwi". What resembled a road before is now more like a river bed and I wondered on the way if it would have been more appropriate to have given Kiwi the name of Pukeko!!!

Many of the smaller bridges have been blown up or washed away and have tree trunks thrown over them for the time being. On one larger bridge the covering planks on both ends have just rotted away leaving only the steel frame. This is all right for the large trucks and buses whose wheels will span the gap but poor little Kiwi's wheels just fitted perfectly 'in' and we were stuck. We had to call on the aid of a few soldiers guarding the bridge to help us lift her out. Then we had to find something to fill in the gap which was easier said than done but eventually we arrived safely on the other side. I gave out some cigarettes to the soldiers who had helped us and told them to be sure and have the bridge mended before we returned but they just laughed from their hammocks (which they hadn't wasted any time in getting back into!!)

On we went, making slow but steady progress. My greatest fear was caused by not knowing the depth of the water we had to go into and I was afraid that our spark plugs would get wet or that we would get stuck in the mud, and if that happened we would have just had to stay put. At one point we had a long wait while one large truck hauling bamboo to Saigon endeavoured to pull another equally large truck out of the 'river'. The water at this particular point was almost level with the floor of the car, but Kiwi swam through it like a fish, with a few prayers to help her along!!

We met our 'friends' again on the way, of course - in fact we had ten encounters with them altogether on the way down. Many of them I remembered meeting on our last trip and mentioned to them that they had been there a long time! They seem to be using the 'friendly' approach now and didn't bother us too much except at one point where Woy was asked in detail the contents of the car and the approx. overall value, and we were informed that we would have to pay them a tax if we made the trip again.

At the following stop we were invited into the house for a drink, which of course we refused and I was subjected to a great speech which was completely lost on me as I couldn't understand a word of it!!! We gave one or two of them a ride down the road so I took the opportunity of pointing out to them the shocking state of the road and suggested that it would be a good idea if they mended it up! I at least got a grunt of a reply! However, friendly as they seemed to be, we were not sorry to leave them behind and sloshed our way on.

Eventually we reached the good road and tried to make up some of the time we had lost, reaching Saigon at about 3 p.m. It was 6.30 p.m. before we had contacted the right people and unloaded our cargo, and we were not sorry to reach our convent in Thi Nghe where we stayed for the night. Actually we had intended spending the following day in Saigon buying up nails, sandpaper, varnish etc., for the workshop but we found that it was a holiday - Armed Forces Day - so there was no purpose in staying. In spite of the protests of the Community we set out on our return trip at 7 a.m. the following morning as we wanted to avoid as much of the hottest part of the day as possible, but the Lord had other ideas!

We were speeding along the good road making great progress for about three-quarters of an hour when suddenly I remembered I had left my bag in the refectory in Thi Nghe!! It contained all my earthly possessions - passport, papers and some money I had drawn from the Bank for the men's wages. What now? Nothing else for it but to turn around and go all the way back. I wondered at the time why the Lord had allowed this to happen and guessed He had something in mind for later on, which He certainly did. This little mishap kept us an hour later than we had intended but we got on the way again feeling a little like St Paul - in perils from robbers, in perils from shipwreck etc. I said a prayer to him and we managed to cope with all the obstacles until we met up again with our 'friends'.

At our first stop we had to take about four of them on board. Three fell in the back and one in the front with us and in spite of his gun he seemed quite friendly! We ended up asking question for question. He'd ask where did I come from so I'd tell him and then ask where he came from, the North or the South but I didn't get an answer. He wanted to know if I was scared of the planes. "Oh no," I replied, "Why would you be scared of the planes?" He didn't answer again but the poor things of course are terrified if they as much as hear a plane as it only means "bombs away" for them. Then he invited us to go and see a film. I didn't quite understand what he was getting at until we rounded a bend and were faced with a long queue of parked trucks and buses, about forty in all. There was nobody in them, only a few Viet Cong (V.C.) walking around about with their guns over their shoulders.

We parted company here with our passengers and Woy and

I decided we could only talk Montagnard from now on and not understand Vietnamese! There was no show of passing so we settled down to wait, thanking God we were an hour late and at the end of the line instead of the front. After about half an hour the people began to return to their vehicles and we were being told by any V.C. who walked down as far as us that we had to go and see this film. You couldn't imagine how convenient it can be at times not to be able to speak a language fluently - as one can then always 'not understand'. We could see the trucks and buses at the top of the queue beginning to move off when a V.C. came down and told me to drive up the road past some of the cars. He ran ahead of me and I was only too pleased to oblige as I could see the chance of getting away. As I drew up beside him he signalled to me to pull over to the other side of the road but I signalled back with a lot of gesticulating that I couldn't because it was too muddy and the car would get stuck.

With this I slipped in between two trucks just beginning to move off and we left him telling his tale of woe to a higher officer who argued back that we DID understand Vietnamese. Woy who had a good sense of humour was nearly bursting to laugh but didn't dare till we were well out of sight, and then we both sat back and enjoyed it to the full. Nothing would have given the enemy more pleasure than to have a picture of me watching their propaganda film. As it was, one of them was working furiously with a movie camera as the cars began to move off. As you can see, this part of the road is still completely under their control. The rest of them on the road didn't bother stopping us now so we were left to cope with the more minor details of the river beds and bridges!! We reached home at 3 p.m. very muddy but very grateful to God for His protection in another eventful trip to the city. You may be wondering what Sister Provincial's reaction to all of this was and so was I. I've just written to tell her I've been!!!

God and Kiwi saw us through many experiences like that. Once we were returning to Phuoc Long when we ran into another attack in which South Vietnam helicopters were engaged. This time we

On the road back from Saigon we watched in horror as the helicopters attacked a nearby enemy unit

stopped and took shelter with some soldiers in a bunker on the side of the road while the helicopters circling overhead rained bullets down, making no distinction between friend or foe. Eventually we were given the all clear and told it was safe to continue on the road. There were young Montagnard boys there whom I knew, only fifteen or sixteen years of age, in fear of their lives, and I was tempted to pile them into the back of the truck and take them home!! They were so frightened and we assured them of our thoughts and prayers on leaving them in the midst of so much danger.

On one occasion we packed up the truck with as much furniture as we could take and I invited two of the men to go down with me. They were handicapped, both victims of the war - one had an artificial leg while the other had only one arm. It was very important that an able-bodied man was not with us because if we were stopped by enemy forces on the road he would have been taken without more ado. On this trip we were held up at one point and the military would not let us through. A battle was being waged somewhere on the road further on. We were there some hours, as once the battle was over the troops had to ensure that the road was cleared of mines etc. Though we had left the mission early, that had not helped us to arrive in Saigon any earlier - we were relieved when we finally got there in the late afternoon. The roads were in some mess with potholes all the way. It was a long, tiring, dusty trip. After a couple of days there, in which time we handed over the furniture to a group of American women for sale, we set out on the return trip. Everything went all right until we reached a small village maybe fifty miles from home.

There we were told that there was a battle being fought further up the road and it would not be safe to carry on until the next day.

I asked the advice of the two men and what they thought we should do as we knew no one in the village and had no-where to stay. While they talked about it I prayed that we would come to the right decision. At 4 pm we decided to carry on and leave our fate in the hands of God who was our best guide. We were warned of the danger of mines on the road that the military had not yet checked for! We put Kiwi into forward gear and I don't think the wheels touched the ground as we strained to see any sign of mines which we would not have had a hope of missing. We didn't stop until we came upon a military outpost where soldiers came out on the road and we had no option but to pull up. Kiwi was mighty glad to have a breather! The soldiers crowded around in disbelief that we had come down the road safely and without being shot at. God was on our side - who could be against us? Great jubilation when we turned up at our front gate as the community were really worried about us, knowing about the battle and not knowing where we were. About that time, the Government sent out an order that all the South houses had to have a flag painted on their roofs, as well as flags flying on any vehicle using the roads, so that the bombers would not attack their own people. We attached two to the bonnet of the truck ready for the next trip we might have to make!!!!

This came about sooner than anticipated and we found ourselves again heading south. We were not far out on the lonely jungle road, this time with a local bus right behind us, when we were pounced on by a group of enemy soldiers - guns, ammunition and all the works! While we were being interrogated and having our nice neat flag ripped off the truck in pure rage, the people in the bus (who knew better than to leave their flags attached in this area) were allowed to pass. Not us, for we blatantly showed that we belonged to the opposition!

We all had to get out of our vehicle and the two men with me had to answer questions. (I being a foreigner would be too stupid to bother with!) Eventually after many warnings we were allowed to continue our journey. One of my men was very shaken as he had been a soldier and left for dead on the battlefield before. He had recovered but his injuries were still very much part of him.

Helicopters and planes were in and out of the Province constantly, especially while the Americans were there in Fire Support Base Buttons. By kindness of the American Army I had many trips by helicopter transport down to Saigon on business. Waiting for them to land and being enveloped in red dust was the only inconvenience.*

Sr. Mary Lawrence

* A fire support base (FSB or firebase) is a military encampment designed to provide artillery support to infantry operating in areas beyond the normal range of fire support from their own base camps. FSBs were used extensively by the U.S. during the Vietnam War.

A military outpost in South Vietnam

Chapter 3

Babies!

On 19th August 1974 two women arrived at the workshop door with a beautiful baby boy, only a few months old I guessed, and asked if I would take him and look after him. Was this a new challenge? Not having had much experience with babies and having no facilities, I suggested that they return home, think about it again, and come back if they really needed to do this. Off they went and I never thought that they would return with the same idea in mind. However, I was proved wrong when they turned up again the following day with the same request.

I needed to know the reason for this plan before I could even consider it. The mother told me that she already had six children to look after and she also needed to work in the rice fields; she was at her wits' end. Her husband was in the army and he agreed with her decision. I could see and understand her predicament. At last I said that we would take the baby until she and her family were in a better situation to take him back.

'Be' with Joey and Paul

We all agreed and so Paul came to stay for the time being. He was actually only a month old and

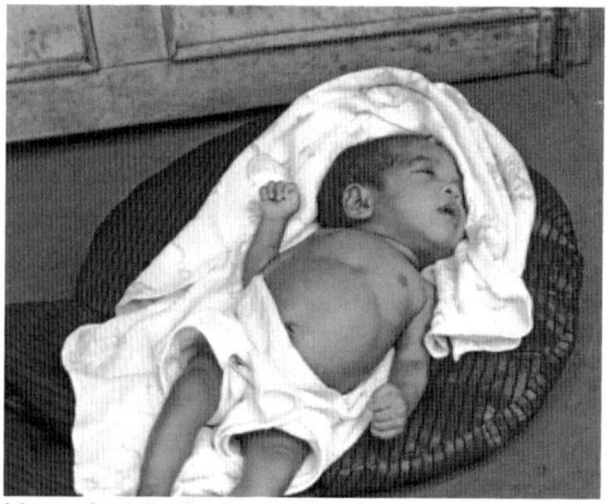
Mary after she had gained weight

weighed four and a half pounds. We had supplies of baby milk powder from New Zealand to help the mothers supplement their supply. Paul gobbled it up and began to grow mightily. I wrote post haste to my mum to ask her to send me a book on how to look after babies, which she duly did. The other problem was where to put him at night. I had a small office in the front of the workshop which was easy to set up and I employed a woman to come in at night to be with him. He was a darling and the Stieng, including my own men, all took a great interest in him and his progress. It turned out to be a good teaching aid for the mothers.

As time went on and word got around about Paul, two more children were brought in to add to the nursery. Joey, aged about five years, was left with us for a short time, and Martha stayed also while we looked after Mary, her little sister. Mary had arrived one afternoon carried in by her older sister, who requested that we look after her. At one glance I could see that the poor wee thing was dying of starvation. They had told me that her mother had died giving birth. I did not think that the baby would live the night through and to avoid any problems that could arise if she died in our care I gave them milk powder and a bottle and told them to come back the following day for more. This they did, but I could see that the baby would not live if she was looked after in the village as there was no clean water or hygiene. So Mary stayed and slowly gained weight and became a great companion for Paul.

Peter was brought in some time about November by his father. He had only been born that morning and his mother had died, so what else could the father do, with other children in the family to look after?

At this stage I had to employ a younger Stieng girl to help with the nursery during the day and Em kept her job as night nurse.

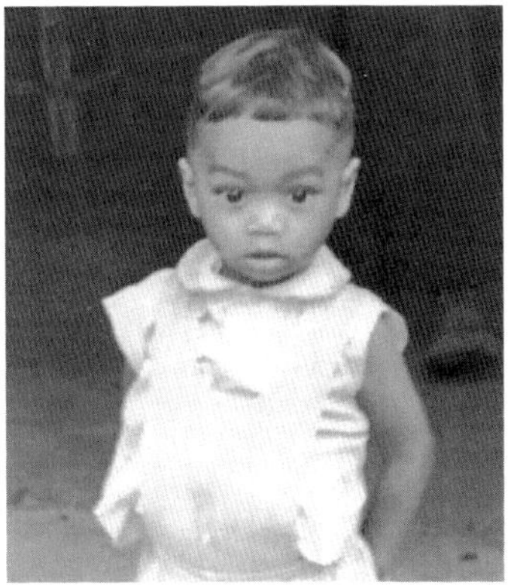
Joey

Monty our monkey fascinated the babies who would sit in their home-made cots by the hour, and watch the antics of Monty in her cage. The men loved the kids and took so much interest in their growth and how we looked after them.

In October 1974 Paul became very ill and I was very frightened he would die on me. He had very bad diarrhoea for a couple of days and when I got him to the doctor on the Saturday afternoon he had a temperature of 102 degrees and was extremely dehydrated. The doctor sent me straight to the hospital to get fluids into him as quickly as possible. I spent all night with him there, and considered my education complete. I stayed on all day Sunday until the drip was finished at 11.30 p.m, and again on the Monday until 10.00 p.m. Paul was now doing fine. Mary also had put on two and a half pounds but I gave a little one who was only two days old back to her mother. When I went out to see her the following week she was in a very poor state, so I suggested that we bring her back home. Sadly, the little girl died that night. We had a small ammunition box which we lined with packing paper and placed the little girl in it for burial.

Chapter 4

The Storm Breaks

In December 1973 I travelled home to New Zealand for a break, which did wonders to restore my spirits. But during that time news was filtering through that the war situation in Phuoc Long was deteriorating. Because it looked as if our area was going to fall to the Communists my holiday was shortened and I returned at the end of January.

Then for no apparent reason at all, the enemy moved out of our area and for the moment things were very quiet, the answer to prayer, undoubtedly.

The next significant event was the Tet, two days of celebration in February for the Vietnamese New Year, when anything was likely to happen. The men all came back to work again, though it took some time to get the rattan and dry it. I had about four days in Saigon before returning to Phuoc Long, so I made good use of the time to pay some overdue visits, lunch with the New Zealand Ambassador and his wife, and a visit to an American in the export business who was interested in helping to market our furniture.

However, our situation soon began to deteriorate when our town came under constant attack again. It was not surprising that on some occasions the enemy stepped up their offensives and made an all-out effort. On one occasion they attacked the military outpost situated on the top of our mountain Nui Ba Ra. The South Vietnamese were up there and would lay mines around the perimeter to stave off attacks. Whether they forgot or were off guard or just did not bother to lay the mines one would never know, but one night the whole camp was attacked and only five men who had hidden managed to survive. The only way to reach the camp was by helicopter and it took about a week to get all the dead brought down to the small local hospital grounds, where they were laid under sheets for families to claim and bury. The trucks were passing our gate for days. Men in gas masks were bringing them in and the terrible stench of death hung over the whole town. Many of these dead were from the tribal villages.

On another occasion there was a big attack on an ethnic village which was on the outskirts of the town. Some of our men were there to halt the enemy and I drove out to see what was happening. They asked me to go back and tell the South Vietnamese commandos that they did not have enough ammunition and what were they to do. I went back and passed on the message, praying all the way that they would get some help. That time they managed to halt the enemy advance during which many enemy soldiers were killed. These were buried in a mass grave which is now a memorial centre for the fallen, many of whom were only young boys.

Life went on each day with its ups and downs and one adapted to the constant shelling and gun fire. Our works went on regardless. We looked for other ways of helping the people and opened up a small stall in the market to sell ethnic artefacts. Unfortunately many people began selling their treasures in order to help their families, ivory ear plugs worn by both men and women, bracelets, rings and ornaments, all handmade from bone, loin cloths woven by hand with intricate designs, anything beautiful or valuable they had.

Helicopters and planes were flying in and out of the Phuoc Binh Province constantly, especially while the American Base was next door.

At the end of October 1974, we were pleased to welcome Sister Dorothy Dixon, another RNDM from New Zealand. After Dorothy had had some time in Saigon learning the language she came to replace Sister Mary Thomas in the dispensary. Another New Zealander, Doctor Margaret Neave from Wellington, a member of the New Zealand medical team in Qui Nhon, also came to help us in this time of transition.

Prior to Christmas Day I had discussed with the families of the children what they wanted us to do if and when the situation got worse. There were only two options, to return the babies to their families, as was the original agreement, or to try and get them to safety. The families realised their inability to nourish and protect the babies as well as themselves under the circumstances. They knew what the outcome would be, so they chose to leave them with us to try to do our best to look after them.

As the situation worsened each day I approached the Chief of Staff, whom I knew well, and asked as a special favour if he could arrange with the next helicopter arrival to take the babies and carers out on the return trip to Saigon. He told me he would do what he could and that we would need to be waiting at the pad which we did in Kiwi, the three babies, two Sisters and their Montagnard carer Nhet. There were crowds of people waiting and hoping as the helicopter landed. By the time the crew had seen to all their business and were ready to take off again my heart sank as no one had given any indication to us to board. I walked over towards the aircraft and a crew member at the door signalled for me to get aboard. I called the others to come quickly and in a matter of seconds we had our precious cargo aboard. We had scarcely jumped down to the ground again when they were airborne. Tears of relief spilled over as we waved them goodbye, thanking God again for His intervention. We were now three, M. Lea, M. Dorothy and myself, and I remember the faces of the people looking at us in disbelief as we walked back to Kiwi. Why hadn't we gone too? Why had we missed a chance like that? I am sure now that they thought we were quite mad. That was supposed to be the last flight in and out.

The men and their families whom we had been trying unsuccessfully to help leave came back to the Mission compound with us where they prepared to stay the night in the workshop under the benches.

The Final Big Offensive On The Town

By December 1974 we could see the situation worsening each day, and many business people in the town began to leave. By then the only way out was by courtesy of the military who were daily flying in provisions, food, guns and ammunition for the army. As each day went on the price paid for a 'space to safety' increased.

The last enemy push came over Christmas. All day Christmas Day we sat on a helicopter pad awaiting the arrival (or hoped-for arrival) of the Chinooks, the big South Vietnamese Army helicopters. Once their cargo was delivered they would return to Saigon otherwise empty.

Recollections of the Battle of Phuoc Long as told by Lt Dam Huu Phuoc, Chief Medic, Tactical Operation Headquarters, 81st Airborne Ranger Group

> *...Colonel Huan, the commander of the 81st Group, made a quick inspection, shook the hand of soldiers and led them into the briefing room where a large battle map of the Phuoc Long town was displayed.*
>
> *As Major Tho, the Section 3 operation officer, swept across the landscape of Phuoc Long with a pointer, our eyes were blurred by the overwhelming red dots representing enemy forces. Blue dots marking friendly forces seemed to be swallowed by this ocean of enemy lines. Phuoc Long is surrounded! The firebase*

at Ba Ra Mountain had fallen into enemy hands. Phuoc Long was dying in the enemy cancer, desperate for the saving hands of the 81st...

...The attack aimed to overtake Phuoc Long started on December 13th, 1974 and on December 21st they seized Song Be airfield.

On December 30th the South Vietnamese Armed Forces counter-attacked to retake the firebase at Ba Ra Mountain. They destroyed sixteen enemy tanks. On January 1st, 1975 the North Vietnamese Armed Forces launched two waves of attacks. With tanks and artillery support they marched into the city of Phuoc Long, but were pushed back by the defensive forces of the Army of Republic of Vietnam. At the Ba Ra Mountain firebase the battle was in favour of the enemy. Phuoc Long was in jeopardy.

Civilians packed around the perimeter of the landing pad desperate to make a final attempt at fleeing the inevitable. On more than one occasion I saw the fear that drove these people, the sheer panic and terror. When each Chinook eventually came to a halt and the blades ceased to rotate, the crew unloaded all that they had and went to negotiate with their counterparts. In that short time the helicopter became crammed with desperate people thinking they were safe. Alas for their hopes! Once the crew returned the intruders were told to get off and when no one obliged they were literally thrown off, baggage and all. We were there with groups of our people who had been warned beforehand not to move until we were sure of a place. How sorry we felt for those so disappointed.

Some of the smaller helicopters took to landing in other places and were taking big money from those who had it, to fly them to safety. Once people heard, they mobbed them too and it was a pitiful sight to see the people hanging on even to the outsides of a helicopter with the rotor going around just above their heads. Christmas Day, the day of peace and goodwill to all peoples!

Sr M. Thomas and me at top of Ba Ra Mountain

Our "bunker" down stairs

While we sat around the landing pad that Christmas Day our attention was drawn to the sky where we saw a huge cargo plane flying out towards Saigon with smoke and flames billowing from the rear. We learned that the pilot had taken off in a direction straight into enemy anti-aircraft guns. Could this be for real?

It was not safe to sleep in the house by this time so we three sisters Dorothy, Lea and I, groups of children and the family who lived on the property, made preparations to wait the night out in the bunkers which had been prepared a long time before. We cooked our rice on a kerosene stove on the path in front of the opening. Our main fear was the shrapnel that flew red hot everywhere when a shell exploded within the vicinity. Many of the men's families came to stay with us in the workshop under the benches for safety. That night tanks began to come up the road behind us firing at the military headquarters in the town in front of us. There we were in between the two forces. I really thought that our end had come. Some time during the night or the early morning we could see a silhouette of a soldier on the wall of the bunker. Friend or foe the grenade could kill us all. We held our breath.

In thc lull in thc fighting which camc with daylight wc managed to extract ourselves from the safety of the depths. We found that the school building down in the garden had been hit and our little house had shell holes through the walls. There was devastation everywhere.

Suddenly we heard people running for their lives up the road at the back of our compound, people in panic running in the direction of the church in the centre of town! What was happening? The only way to know was to follow, so we set out for the church where a great number of people had congregated. It appeared enemy soldiers had forced their way into the homes of the people living in a valley below the town and the people were sure they would either be bombed by the south military or killed by the enemy. They had come to the priest for guidance.

The poor priest was supposed to know what to tell them to do! The poor man was at his wits' end so I offered to go over to the military H.Q. situated across the road to tell them of the situation and ask them what civilians should do. The officers there were all underground with their radio equipment but I knew the Chief of Staff and asked for instructions. He advised the priest to tell the people to go home if they had a bunker to get into; if not, to stay in the church. I went back and delivered the message just as shells began to bombard us again, and Dorothy and I took cover under our small Hilux van. The priest gave everyone general absolution before we made tracks back to the mission.

The following morning after another night in the bunker we realised that we could not stay there safely any longer. We put on our packs that we had always had ready for such an occasion, and prepared to move out to the valley with the people who were left. (We did not know until much later that overnight the church had received a direct hit and many people had been killed).

> *On January 3rd, 1975 the North Vietnamese Armed Forces stepped up their attack; they bombarded the city of Phuoc Long with more than 3000 rounds of artillery.*

The only date I remember was the day we left the mission, January 3rd, 1975. Before setting out Lea distributed the Blessed Sacrament and we left the chapel in order for our return. The children and the family came with us, and we joined the population of the town, making our way down to the river and across the bridge to the valley. Here we spent the rest of that day and that night on an open grassy side of the hill. We did not know at that stage that communist forces were on top of the opposite hill with their guns ready to fire across to the town.

That night many of us grabbed what sleep we could, lying on the ground in the open with our heads resting on our packs. The following morning I went in search of the men, hoping they could guide us through the jungle to the next Province and safety. I sat down with a group of them and we had just begun making a plan when all the

guns in creation started blasting all around us. Who would know where they were coming from?

In a flash the men (who had all been soldiers) were up and gone, for they knew the danger and I did not. When I found myself left high and dry I decided to make my way back to our own group but that necessitated some time in a gully lying on the ground while shells and shrapnel fell all around us. A group of Vietnamese had been close to where we had been and one poor woman had been hit with shrapnel from head to toe. How easily it could have been me! They carried her further on and I stayed with her, trying to pray and not finding a word. She died there with no medical help whatsoever.

Eventually I reached our group again and panic had broken out. Bullets were audible as they flew past our heads. People were coming to us for shrapnel wounds as we were the only ones who had any medical supplies. We heard that most of the hospital staff had got away by helicopter. A man then came to ask for help for a soldier in a house on the other side of the bridge. I went with him on the back of his motorbike while the others stayed and did what they could for the wounded. Their numbers were growing by the minute.

I went into the house to be confronted by a young Vietnamese soldier lying on a table. At first sight there was little evidence of any injury but another soldier was trying desperately to dislodge a clot from the patient's windpipe with his fingers. I immediately saw the futility of that - the poor young fellow had a shrapnel wound on the side of his nose and there must have been massive internal bleeding which was now choking him. I did what I could and suggested that they move him so that his head lay back to allow a straight line to his lungs. His poor wife was there pleading, "He won't die, will he?"

What could I say? I went outside and had to sit down for a while. I heard someone say, "She is tired with too much to do". I realised then that we had not eaten since the morning before. I got back on

The only surviving photo's of our exodus with the people

the motorbike and the man took me back to the others. The rest of that day is a blur, with people coming and wanting to take us to their wounded. In the end I suggested to some of the men that they build a shelter and bring us all the wounded there together to save time. The battle went on all that day over our heads, and all sorts of rumours went around about reinforcements being parachuted in. If that was truc it proved to be too late. Some military were around but I had no idea what they were doing.

> *Rescue forces were deployed to Phuoc Long by air at 8.00 a.m. that same day. About an hour later they circled in the sky above Phuoc Long but failed to land under enemy attack from the ground. The rescue forces had to return to Long Binh.*
>
> *By 7.00 p.m. on January 6th, 1975, Phuoc Long had completely fallen.*
>
> *The fate of Phuoc Long foreshadowed the fall of South Vietnam. Without strong military and political leader support how could a few committed soldiers save the cause of an entire country?*

By about 4.00 p.m. it was evident that we were in the wrong place, military on both sides were firing across us and many shells were falling short. No one seemed to be taking charge of the situation as far as the civilians were concerned so I collared a soldier and demanded that they, the military, help to take the people to somewhere safer. He looked at me as though I was from another planet and told me to take them along a road which I knew led to nowhere! He added that the people would not be able to follow the soldiers into the jungle because of the difficulties!

By 5.00 p.m. we had spread the word to follow the military. Our dilemma now was whether we ourselves would stay with the wounded or go with the people. We decided on the latter because there was little we could do for the wounded without a doctor, supplies or needed expertise. Maybe we could be of more use to those who could still move.

The exit wound up over the hill behind us and out into we knew-not-where. It was a matter of following the person in front of you in blind faith. By 7.00 p.m. night had fallen and no one knew where we were. We stopped and prepared to settle down right there until daylight. Using our packs for pillows again we tried to get some sleep.

In the morning none of us, nor any one around us, knew which way to go, so because of this we discussed our predicament and finally decided to go back to where we had been. What was the purpose of wandering around in circles? At that precise moment a Government official arrived and encouraged us to keep going. In his words, "It is finished. You can't go back!" So we donned our packs again and set out, following the trail left by those who had gone before us into the jungle. Not far along we had to wade through mud in a swampy area and many lost their sandals. Feet came up from the bog minus sandals and there was nothing people could do to find lost footwear in the deep mud. Luckily Dorothy and I had foreseen something like this in planning for emergencies and a few weeks earlier we had both bought ourselves basketball boots from the market. These proved to be invaluable now as we were able to tie the laces firmly.

Gradually we caught up with others ahead of us, as more joined the ranks behind. What a pathetic single line of humanity trudging into the unknown, desperately hoping that this would be better than the known! My heart still goes out to those who carried their loved ones on their backs, those who would not leave them behind just because they had already been wounded. One young man in particular carried his wife up hill and down dale and we always knew when they were close by from the stench of her wounds. The fear and anguish etched on their faces told it all.

We walked, slipped, scrambled in single file through rivers and streams. One of them I am sure was part of the Song Be river. There we used the rocks above the rapids as stepping stones, knowing that a slip or over-balance would carry us downstream to certain death. By the time we reached the other side the climb up the incline was already a slide of wet mud. Women and children managed to cling to the slope out of sheer terror and desperation.

It was out there that we learned of the destruction of the church the night before and the deaths of those who had taken shelter there. The poor priest, they said, was now a wreck himself after burying them all. We also heard from some of the men who were close by that some of the villages on top of a strategic hill had been bombed and many people killed. Among those dead was an old friend, one of the first men who had come to work with me at the very beginning of the workshop who had helped to make all the bricks we had needed. Both his legs had been blown off.

We trudged all day and only when nightfall came did our long stumbling crocodile stop. Now the cold of the jungle set in. We lit fires both to keep warm and to boil some water. One thing that I had included in my backpack was some teabags which kept me going when the cold rice became too difficult to swallow. I will never forget the kindness of the people. I was deeply touched and tears still come to my eyes when I remember how one of our Stieng men brought us rice already cooked in a bamboo according to their method, rice that he could not afford to give away. Another woman, a business woman from the town who was the last of her family to leave, had carried warmer clothing with her and when she saw us in our thin smocks offered us one of her warm coats to throw over us during the night. How thankful we were! Only the best in people comes out at such times.

All this time planes flew overhead and the warning to douse our fires as they approached soon became routine. If a light of any kind had been spotted we would have been bombed by our own forces for they would have been unable to distinguish us from the enemy. Sometimes as we moved on we would find messages tacked on the trees along the path telling us to be very quiet since we were very close to an enemy camp. I remember one man carrying his child who began to cry, and the struggle that he had to smother the cries.

We still did not know where we were going and only hoped that those ahead did. Sometimes in the mornings when we 'came to' after an exhausted sleep, oblivious to the creatures crawling around us on the ground, as well as snakes up the trees over our heads, we would hear the ring of a bell. For some time it puzzled us until it turned out to be the enemy camp waking up their men! Each day we struggled on, waking every morning feeling weaker and more tired from the lack of food.

My Silver Jubilee of Religious Profession came at this time and during one of the rest times in the day the three of us celebrated on what was left of the cold rice. My thoughts were with the other ten Sisters of our group celebrating far away back home in New Zealand. I wondered if they were thinking of us.

One evening as we huddled around our small fire trying to keep warm a Stieng man came over and asked if we could help his child who was very ill. I suggested that he bring the child to us as we could see better by the light of the fire. This he did, carrying a little boy of four or five years old in his arms. As soon as we saw the child we realised that he was already dead. The difficult part was telling that to the father, poor man. Once the family knew what had happened they began the customary wailing. We should have stopped them at once for fear that the enemy would hear but I did not have the heart. They wailed on as they prepared to bury their little boy there in the middle of the jungle where we were camped. I prayed that the little fellow would guide and protect us as we journeyed on and comfort his poor family.

By this time things were beginning to get a bit blurry. All I could think of now was the ordeal of putting one leg in front of the other as we trudged on. When would we ever stop? We came to a swamp that seemed to block our way forwards, and there seemed nothing else for it but to plunge into the sea of grey mud that sucked at our feet and made it almost impossible to pull one out to take the next step. Black roots of whatever reached their heads upwards and made us wonder what our feet were touching underneath! While we were still engaged in this battle with the swamp we came face to face with another group of people going in the opposite direction, back to where we had come from. They told us that they had been stopped further on by North Vietnamese troops who ordered them to turn around and go back again. These people encouraged us to go with them but the prospect of trudging all that way again didn't really appeal. We would rather face the enemy, we thought.

We finally extracted ourselves from the last of the knee-deep mud only to find to our horror that our legs, feet and boots were full of leeches. This greatly amused our two small boys who stood looking and laughing at us. Ridding ourselves of the swamp mud was bad enough but getting rid of the leeches was another thing. Not being smokers ourselves Lea, Dorothy and I had to borrow a lighter and burn them off one by one. This took a while but gave us time just to be able to revel in the luxury of sitting!

Days and nights went by as we trudged on. We had to discourage people from sitting down during the day. The danger now was that they would not have the strength to get up again. At one stage we came across a clearing and a young Vietnamese woman in front told us that it was a Communist road through the jungle. We would have to run for our lives to get across it. The fear, of course, was that we would be machine-gunned in the process and we would have no cover. Whether or not we ran, I cannot remember now. Somehow we safely managed to reach the other side and the protection of the jungle again, much to our relief.

Late one morning as we pushed on we came upon groups of people ahead of us just sitting down and saying nothing. They looked completely finished. Immediately I started to encourage them to get up, it wouldn't be much further now! As I moved along the line I became aware of a figure in black with rubber sandals on, leaning against a tree watching us. I knew then why everyone had stopped. There were North Vietnamese Communist Army Forces around us. I thought quickly and just kept walking as if I had not seen him. Just as I was about to pass him he put the barrel of his gun out in front of me and I had no option but to stop. One doesn't fight against a loaded gun. So we sat down, too, but not for long. By this time any idea of days or nights had merged and I could not say how long we had been moving by then.

Chapter 5

Prisoners

Actually by this time I was struggling to keep on putting one foot in front of the other. I didn't care now who stopped us, as long as we could sit down. At one stage I had seen on a rise in front of us our two little boys looking back at us and laughing. I didn't know till later that they were laughing at me as I struggled drunkenly ahead.

The Communist soldier in charge of us now wanted to move us on directly but we played for time, saying that we needed to have something to eat. We messed around for as long as we could, trying to swallow cold rice, but his patience began to run out. It was best not to antagonize him further. It was at this point that Lea, Dorothy and I were taken from the people and separated from the children who cried bitterly. The two boys were ahead of us and separated from the other children. Being boys of course they could be used in many ways by the military so they were allowed to accompany us. As we set off we collected two or three South Vietnamese army prisoners who were roped together to accompany us on this part of the journey.

We were marched off under guard for the rest of that day until we arrived in a banana grove. There we camped for the night on banana leaves on the ground while the other prisoners, being men and always superior to women, were allowed the raised platform in a

Original sketch courtesy of Sr. M. Philippa Rood

hut formerly used by plantation growers. We must have slept well. When we awoke in the morning M. Dorothy told how she had felt something in her hair during the night and when we investigated we found she had been sleeping over the entrance to a field-mouse's hole. We were all very tired and our feet covered in blisters so we were not able to walk at the pace of the fresh guards. This did not please them at all. I got really angry when one of them shoved M. Lea with his rifle across her back, nearly causing her to fall. Sister had malaria at this stage and was trying to struggle along as best she could with all her baggage. At one point, much to our relief, we had a change of guards. I asked the fresh one if he would help Sister and carry her bag for her. This he kindly did without further ado, God bless him.

After another day of walking we arrived at our first prison camp, in Quang Duc. When the commander saw us three nuns, two foreigners, American for sure! and one Chinese he was floored. The Communists did not want us there; in fact I think they did not know what to do with us. I asked M. Lea who was our spokesperson to implore them to let us stay there, at least until we had a rest. After much deliberation they took us down to the remnants of a house consisting of six uprights and the remains of some thatch on the roof. We fell on the ground and immediately fell asleep. Bliss! We woke up later to find a group of military standing around gaping at us.

This camp turned out to be a prison set up for the soldiers they had captured from Phuoc Long. There was a high bamboo fence separating us from the men, with huts inside the enclosure. Outside the enclosure were piles of boots taken from the prisoners before they were locked inside. We found out later the reason for that. We were told not to try to run away, (very unlikely in the state that we were in), as there were bamboo stakes in the ground all around the camp which would pierce right through our feet if trodden on. We were content for the moment to stay put. The night was still very cold so we lit a fire and were pleased to have it to ward off the clutches of insects making a good meal out of us. The night dragged on and we wondered how the people and the children were faring. When it rained, the only cover we had was a groundsheet, not very big and not really rainproof.

The following morning we requested the commander to give us a platform on which to lie at night away from the damp insect-ridden ground. He duly obliged and sent some of the prisoners out to cut bamboo. In no time we had a platform on which to sit, lie or just be so we had at least that little comfort. As night came on again so did the cold. We soon learnt that newly cut bamboo can be very cold, and the night was spent huddling up to one another under the small groundsheet. By morning we had slept little and we welcomed the rising sun with its warmth.

The following days we spent explaining the reasons and functions of everything in our pack to our interrogators. One item that gave me a considerable amount of trouble was a flare gun which I had procured long before and which I had never used, principally because I didn't know how to! I spent hours explaining it away but it was hard to convince them that it wasn't a piece of weaponry to be used against them. They wanted to know all that we were doing in Phuoc Long and the people whom we knew there. They seized on my little address book and minutely went through every address I had in it, and especially those of American army personnel. I had to account for every one I knew, who they were, what they did and how I knew them. Finally they ended up asking me, didn't I know they were all CIA?

So the day went on until the afternoon came and we were concerned how to survive the night. We collected sticks and branches, whatever was available nearby, until we thought we had enough to keep the fire going all night. Rice again for the meal! I tried to see if there was enough space under the platform for the fire to burn without burning the bamboo. To our delight this little scheme worked well and all night we were kept warm to hot as we roasted above on the bamboo rack over our small fire. Sometimes it even got too hot so I had to pull the coals out from underneath for a while, and when the temperature dropped again, back went the fire. Stoking up the furnace had nothing on this!

So we survived and began to regain our strength slowly. One of the worst things that happened in these first few days was the arrival of the commander who demanded that the two little boys who were still with us be taken and held somewhere else. The poor kids cried, and we cried too until we knew in no uncertain terms that this had to be. The boys left us reluctantly and I often wonder where they ended up, probably as child soldiers helping the cause. We never saw or heard of them again.

We lost our watches, our camera, book of prayers which we recite daily and everything other than our clothing (or what was left of it). When we saw that these confiscated things were not going to be returned to us I asked one of the soldiers if I could have my watch back as we didn't have any way of telling the time or keeping track of the days. I asked also for my prayer book, and was surprised to have both returned over the following days. In the Office were my only spiritual helps for each day. There was always a special message that fitted in with what was happening and gave courage and consolation in the fact that we were not alone but God was with us in a very tangible way on this weird journey.

The guards kept their eyes well on us and we were frequently visited by military personnel who wanted all the information they could get about us, where we came from, our childhood, our schooling, school exams, what our fathers did, how many in the family, our income, date of entering religious life, teaching career, date of coming to

Vietnam, everything up until that day. It all had to be in writing so it gave us something to do, our life history. Each day the interrogations continued, one day on a very friendly note, the next shouting and accusing. We had to be careful that our replies were consistent and truthful otherwise they would trip us up easily.

After we had been in the camp some time and the daily interrogations were easing off the 'powers that be' asked if we would like to visit some of the people that we had left on the track. We of course eagerly agreed and were taken through the jungle to a village manned by the North Vietnamese. There we found that many of our people had been placed in with these families to be kept under strict control and interrogation. We managed to get a few questions with some. They told us they were being held and could not talk quietly to one another without every word being overheard. In spite of all our problems, though, it was good to meet again and give and receive courage, all very quietly!

Each day we were given enough rice to last us for the day. We cooked it ourselves, each taking a daily turn. Once we began to recover from our tiredness I began to feel the effects of the lack of sustaining food. The prisoners were given casava* to cook and unbeknown to the guards I would beg some off them when they were preparing it. I had an anchor milk powder tin in which I had kept the precious tea bags; now we used it to make a casava pudding, which tasted the same as casava chips or boiled casava, whichever the cook preferred to experiment with.

There was a stream running through the area where we could wash and collect water to boil for drinking. We shared the precious tin when we needed a drink as we had no such luxury as a mug or cup.

When we had left home M. Lea had carried the history of the house and other important papers with her. After begging her to leave it all behind, knowing it was a burden for her to carry, one day I had

* Casava A woody shrub with edible tuberous roots - a good source of carbohydrates.

actually thrown it away, but not far enough to prevent her from retrieving it. When we arrived at this first camp and had a fire going she herself had quietly burned everything to prevent it ever being taken and used against us. As the days dragged on, for how long it would be, we had no idea, we badly wanted to keep some kind of record of what was happening but we dared not. Our captors were so suspicious and nervous that even names and dates committed to paper without their express authorisation could have cost us our lives.

Faithful little Bobby was still with us. Once on our arrival at the camp Bobby had barked at the soldiers when they came near us, and one of the guards told us if the dog barked he would shoot it. Bobby must have been listening in too, he never barked again in that camp.

After perhaps ten days at the 'holding pen' we were told we would be moved somewhere else destination unknown. In one way we were sorry to leave because we knew many of the prisoners on the other side of the enclosure and were able to have a word or two with them at times on the quiet. Their primitive toilet arrangement was outside the fence and when they needed to use it they had to ask the guard to let them out. The guards were not too gracious at these times and would let the prisoners know their annoyance, especially those unfortunate enough to be suffering from diarrhoea. I felt our presence there was a deterrent for bad treatment and wondered how the prisoners would fare when we left.

One morning we had to walk under guard to a wide dirt road in the middle of nowhere where an army jeep was waiting for us. The three of us piled into the back seat with Bobby on the floor under our feet. He had never been in a vehicle before and was overcome with car sickness at one stage but we never said a word.

On this road we met large army trucks filled with soldiers and army equipment all covered in green leaves and branches as camouflage from the South Vietnamese planes trying to spot any movement from above. Our jeep stopped whenever we heard a plane and we too were covered with branches. At one point we arrived at the banks of a wide river with a steep incline on the other side. How were we going to get through this? Much to our consternation the driver just kept going right into the water then we chugged out safely on to the other side. A bridge of rocks had been built under the water! It would never have been spotted from the air, and the vehicles, all being army, had no trouble in driving through and climbing the muddy incline on the other side. We travelled like this all day until we entered a rubber plantation. Weaving our way around the rubber trees we eventually arrived at our destination as darkness fell.

On the inside cover of my prayer book I had written inconspicuously *9th January 1975 Thursday Arrival at "Open Air Hillside Retreat"*.

What a step up in accommodation standards! Here we found ourselves housed in a small thatched hut with three raised platforms for beds, and even mosquito nets. What luxury! There was a small table in the middle with tiny Chinese cups and saucers and teapot. I can't remember if there was anything in the teapot, we were too tired to care by that time and were not at all interested in sightseeing in the dark. We were just glad of a place to lay our heads. Bobby curled up on the dirt floor and kept guard.

The next morning we found that we were in a small compound consisting of our little hut and what had been the guards' accommodation. All around us were fields of casava which would have been a nice variation from the diet of rice, but we were warned against approaching this, much less pulling any up to cook. We took turns at cooking once a day and collecting the wood needed. Any rice left from the meal we would hang from the roof, covering it with a tin plate. This was to protect it mainly from insects and at night from the rats which would come down from the thatched roof. Often they woke us up with the clattering of the plates as they tried to get at thc rice. Poor M. Lea had to get up and try to frighten the rats away while Dorothy and I prayed that she would accomplish the task satisfactorily. I can remember how very weak I was from the lack of food. I went to collect wood one day. Bringing in a few sticks took me about twenty minutes and left me completely exhausted.

One interrogator, a young soldier, spoke very good English with an English accent and I asked him where he had learnt it. He replied, "From the radio". Another day I told him that I felt sorry for him and he asked why. I replied that he had no God to whom he could turn. He made no reply to that and I didn't labour the point.

The days dragged on in that fashion with no sign of release. At one stage we could hear bombing by planes not too far distant and the guards showed us a bunker into which to go if we were directly attacked. We were also told to take any clothing off an old clothes line if we heard the approach of planes. They told us that we would come to no harm unless we received a direct hit! Thankfully we never had to use the bunker. Later we found out and saw for ourselves the remains of a town, Dong Xoai, which had been bombed by the South in retaliation for the fall of Phuoc Long.

We spent each day in prayer and sharing with M. Lea all that was going on; she picked up news which we were missing because of our limited knowledge of Vietnamese. Dorothy made some very good pois from the dried leaves of the banana tree and we practised doing the poi dance* to help while away the time.

With our diet so very limited we were desperate for some sugar. We found a small bush growing nearby with small flowers similar to the passionfruit flower. We tried some of the berries and they gave us a small taste of sweetness. A few times our guards came to offer us a chicken. The problem was that the poor chicken was still alive and we would have to start from scratch! The only one who was brave

*Poi dance: A traditional Maori dance performed while rythmically swinging a ball on a cord.

enough to kill it was M. Lea who valiantly took on the unpleasant task. We helped with the plucking and cleaning and waited for the meat to be ready. No matter how long we boiled the chickens we still had difficulty chewing the meat because of its toughness. We tried doing it a few times until at last poor M. Lea refused to kill one more bird. When the next chicken arrived I decided to make a little cage for it and wait for it to lay us an egg! When it didn't oblige we let it go. I still have one of the few feathers I saved as a keepsake.

One day after a few weeks there we heard the sound of a radio down in the guards' house. We had been starved of outside news for so long it acted as a magnet (which it was intended to do). I moved closer and heard a 'News Program'. We learnt later that it had all been for our benefit and was probably on a tape recorder. The startling news was that Saigon had fallen and the New Zealand Embassy was no more. It never occurred to me not to believe it at the time, so ignorant were we in every way.

We were visited many times by army officials who didn't seem to do anything other than accuse me of being a CIA agent! There were more interrogations. We had no papers or passports. We'd taken the precaution of sending them on to safety in Saigon and now we were pestered for personal information.

I could have passed myself off as Irish; my parents were both Irish, having emigrated to New Zealand in 1926 and Ireland was a neutral country in this war. But since all my growing up and schooling had been in New Zealand, I stuck to New Zealand. My father was a railway worker. That seemed to please them, I was therefore working class. (I did not mention that he was also a cattle-dealer as a side-line.) Poor Sister Dorothy was treated with contempt. She had said that her father ran a hotel, capitalist proprietor that he was, of a modest little hotel in the small country town of Opotiki! They even asked me what my brothers' incomes were. I laughed then, picturing my brothers' reactions if I'd ever thought to ask them that.

One evening out of the blue we were invited to watch a film with a number of people we had never seen before. It was a film of the fall of Phuoc Long after we left, and the raising of the communist flag over what had been the Province Chief's house. It wasn't something we needed to see. We knew only too well that civilians and military who were our friends had died for this. They also showed captured U.S. troops being interrogated and their replies, praising the way in which they were being treated.

The next day we were all taken into a hut with white sheets hanging around to give it the impression of a room. Here we were interrogated in front of video cameras and our replies to questions recorded. They made sure of course that we replied in a "favourable manner".

It's a long road to freedom

Chapter 6

FREEDOM!

A day or two after all that, we were told to be ready in the morning to leave the camp at 4.00 a.m. Our 'friends' were going to release us! We were overjoyed of course and spent the rest of the night getting ready though we had nothing to get ready with! Days and nights had merged into one since leaving our Mission and it wasn't until later that we realised we had been in captivity for at least seven weeks. Early the next morning we were told to wear our full religious habits. We had been wearing a grey smock and veil, all that we had, apart from the habits we were trying to keep clean by not wearing them. I had no intention of spending the next day in an old army jeep, covered in dust and clothed to my neck in the heat so I took no notice of the "orders" and put on my old grey smock. On inspection in the morning the 'powers that be' refused to move until I was fully and formally clothed. Bobby knew something was going on and joined in the excitement.

At this stage, they brought our belongings that had been confiscated when we arrived, minus the flare gun and all the medicines that we had carried. They did return my camera, with film included, and I was hopeful that I would now have all the photos I had taken on our journey. (This however, was not meant to be as the film had been deliberately exposed - more about that later).

We left in a convoy of jeeps and drove for a couple of hours to a large house which would have belonged to a rubber plantation owner. I don't know who was there but we were invited upstairs for breakfast. Could this be for real? We were given boiled eggs and bread that must have been more than three months old at least. It was so hard that we were lucky to break a piece off. We had to thump it vigorously to try to remove the ants making hay in each hole in the loaf! It was such a crackly mess that, hungry as I was for bread, I could only manage one mouthful.

After 'breakfast' we were taken into the remains of the town that had been bombed, as mentioned before. Nothing had been left standing and there were rows of graves along the road where the dead had been buried. What useless destruction of lives. Our captors took us into what remained of the church, the few walls still standing cracked and dangerous to be near. The next thing that I remember was a microphone being shoved in front of me while I was asked, "What do you think of this and the American oppression?" All I could say was, that war is no solution to any of the world's problems, and left it at that. We were glad to leave the poor little village with its dead, and with little hope for the living. I was surprised to note that the rubber processing plant was still untouched and working.

From there we travelled on all day except for a break at one stage, in what I would have presumed was the remains of a neat little French bungalow. Eventually, about 4.00 p.m. we stopped on an old road I recognised that I had travelled before when going to Saigon. We were glad to get out and stretch our legs.

At this point cameras came to light from nowhere, and we were videoed and photographed being farewelled by the officials. Some we knew and some we had never seen before. Before we took our leave, we were warned that we would have to walk on our own from that point and if anything happened to us on the way they would not be responsible.

Out came our precious camera to record this wonderful occasion. We had no idea then that the film had been tampered with and replaced carefully.

The start of our long walk to freedom

M. Lea and myself with Bobby started out on the road while Dorothy made use of the camera. Hardly daring to believe that we were actually free we sang "it's a long, long road to freedom". I struggled out of my dirty habit to put on my cooler smock, with little thought of any danger that might still be ahead of us.

After walking for more than two hours and not really knowing our destination, we saw a military look-out post and came into the small South Vietnamese village of Nuoc Vang, in the District of Phu Giao. Military personnel stopped us and we had to explain who we were and where we had come from. They told us that they had been expecting us. A US helicopter had been waiting to fly us somewhere but it had gone because of our late arrival.

We were escorted then to the parish priest's house where we stayed for the night, the priest being away at the time. I cannot remember a housekeeper or anyone else being there. By the time we found our way around and lit some kerosene lamps it would have been about 7.30 p.m. I had a terrible craving for a banana and suggested that we go down the road to see if there were any to buy. We were a source of great curiosity to the local village people. Much to our joy we found a woman with a stall on which there were different-sized bananas for sale. Dorothy's choice was a medium-sized one, but I in my craving wanted the biggest there was. Off we went back to the house with our prize, but consternation! My banana turned out to be full of seeds.

Our beds that night were the ordinary Vietnamese type, of hardboard slats. Normally one would have a mat over them. We were wishing for the bamboo beds which we had got used to during our captivity.

The following morning we were picked up by military jeep again, supposedly on our way to a hospital, but we stopped somewhere to visit some of our people. I remember well a Stieng woman who recognised me coming over and hugging me. She was so pleased to see that we were still alive, and we wept in each other's arms. I found many people there whom we knew but did not have time to stay long enough to find answers to all the questions I wanted to ask.

At some time during that day we drove into the grounds of a large hospital run by the Sisters of St Paul de Chartres, in Binh Duong. We stayed there, and as time went on we began to wonder just what was going on. At some stage I looked out of a window and saw people milling around outside - TV cameras and journalists. What was all this about? Then the penny dropped. We were now prisoners of the South, who wanted to hear our story and make sure that we had developed no sympathy with the enemy. We were thrilled and surprised when a group of Sisters arrived from our convent in Thu Duc, overjoyed to find that we were safe and back in the land of the living again. That was truly a wonderful reunion and I was so pleased to reunite Bobby with his former mistress, Sister M. Christiane, who took him home with her in their car - a step up from what he had got used to. Eventually a New Zealand Embassy representative, Frank Wilson, arrived to claim and collect us. He had to sign a paper that we had been handed over in good condition, but still the authorities did all in their power to prevent the car from leaving. We were sorry that M. Lea could not accompany us that night, as the Chinese Embassy had yet to claim her. (She reached our convent in Thu Duc the following day).

Even though we were picked up by an official Embassy car it was not easy for us to leave the hospital. The Vietnamese did not want us to go, probably thinking that we might spread "good news" of the enemy. The journalists also tried to block our way. We breathed a sigh of relief when the car was able to move out on our way to the Embassy, the same Embassy we'd been told by radio news was long ago abandoned!

It was late in the afternoon when we reached Saigon and Frank, the First Secretary of the Embassy, rang through to New Zealand so that we could talk with our families. What a thrill for us and for my Mum who had shown such faith in me all the way through. Unfortunately Dorothy could not contact her father immediately but did so the following day somewhere in the Bay of Plenty. We were then driven out to our Sisters, and what a homecoming and celebration that was! Once we had hugged every Sister, I was anxious to be reunited with the three babies and their carer Nhet. We found them in the nursery looking so well and thanked God that they had not been with us in our ordeal. Mail and parcels had accumulated over Christmas for us. What a thrill to unwrap Christmas cake cooked and sent by Mum, the very thing I had dreamed of so often in the jungle!

After a few days with our Sisters it became evident that the journalists were not going to leave us alone. The Sisters were anxious that we might cause a problem for them too, so we took ourselves off to our Sisters in Nha Trang where no one knew us or bothered about us. Sitting on the beautiful beach each day and watching people going about their daily lives seemed so unreal. Was this the same country I was in? Did these people know what was going on only a few miles away? Unbelievable! We enjoyed our time there, it was another world. At that point we travelled over to Qui Nhon and stayed the weekend with the New Zealand medical team who treated us royally before we returned to Saigon.

There were many things I wanted to do. The major concern was to find out what had happened to our people while we were being held. American officials were still operating and many friends were around who were always willing to give a hand when they could.

I also still had that film in my camera which I wanted to get developed. I couldn't believe my good luck in having it returned but I soon learned the truth, it had been exposed and put back as if nothing had happened. I was very disappointed but thankful that not all had been lost - we had three good snaps, the first and the last two.

There were many friends in Saigon who needed to be contacted so the first week back was taken up renewing acquaintance. One of these was American Catholic Relief Services from whom I borrowed a motor-bike on which to get around.

Eventually I arranged through an American office to fly up to a remote town by helicopter to find some of our refugees who had managed to get through to the border. I was looking forward so much to this reunion but on arrival found that there had been an attack close by and I could not get out to the camp.

Soon refugees were pouring down through the country more than ever as one town after another was attacked and taken over. Camps were set up for these people but they were a long way out of the city and we needed transport to get there. I knew that New Zealand was a member of the International Red Cross so I took off on my motor bike and arrived at the Red Cross centre, just another foreigner in a helmet! I found an office that looked hopeful and asked across the counter if I could borrow a Red Cross van. They looked at me in amazement, wondering what planet I had just arrived from, but at least they started asking questions before they dismissed me.

When I told the officer my name, the penny dropped. Apparently our capture had featured on the news and our release-pictures had been on TV, and that worked wonders. I think that I could have had as many vans as I'd wanted. I drove out with my motor bike in the back, secretly hoping that this old vehicle with a Red Cross on both sides would last long enough to get us to where we needed to go.

HỘI HỒNG - THẬP - TỰ
VIỆT - NAM CỘNG - HÒA

Trụ sở:
201, đường Hồng-Thập-Tự
SAIGON

Điện-thoại: 22,298 - 91.710

Số 466/75 HTT/TU

Put at the disposal of Sister W. Laurence, New Zealand Notre Dame des Missions, Hoàng-Diệu St. Thu-Đức,

a LAND ROVER No 039

to be used and taken care of by herself for refugees in An-Lợi, Long-Thành.

The car should be sent to Red Cross for checking twice a week and gazeline is to be afforded by Sister Laurence.-

Saigon, April 1st, 1975

Sister W. Laurence

Mr Phan-văn-Nhàn
Vice President

LETTERS TO MUM:

Nha Trang

7th March 1975

…I have made arrangements with the Americans here to get a flight into Quang Duc on Wednesday where I am told 1600 of our Montagnards have managed to get to…

13th March

…could not get to Quang Duc yesterday on account of new wave of fighting in that province. Very disappointed…

Thi Nghe

9th April

…have just finalised arrangements to have sixteen of our orphans in Thu Duc taken to Australia on their next air lift…

With funds that had accumulated in the bank from generous donors, mostly in New Zealand, and with our van, we were in a good position to help the refugees. Once we had found where the camps were and were able to see the basic needs, we set about buying up - mugs, tin plates and chopsticks plus quantities of bush knives with which the men could cut bamboo and improve their meagre shelters. Cooking utensils were also scarce so these we also managed to provide from the roomy back of the van.

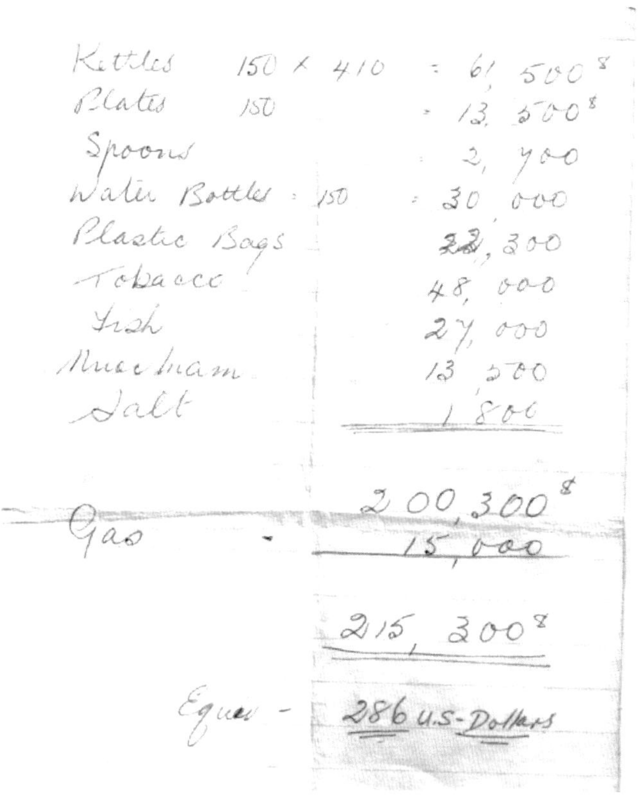

Kettles	150 × 410	= 61,500$
Plates	150	= 13,500$
Spoons		= 2,700
Water Bottles	= 150	= 30,000
Plastic Bags		22,300
Tobacco		48,000
Fish		27,000
Nuoc mam		13,500
Salt		1,800
		200,300$
Gas		15,000
		215,300$
Equiv -		286 U.S-Dollars

The list of supplies from my notebook

Visiting refugees outside Saigon after our release.
There were 27,000 people in this camp in An Loi alone!

Everyone took it for granted that we were working with the Red Cross and sometimes that acted in our favour. I remember one occasion when we were driving into one of the camps and we heard gun shots close by. We saw a man fall to the ground by the side of the road. We pulled up and while the poor man was being loaded into the van we were asked to take him to the hospital somewhere in the vicinity. It appeared that the chap was a soldier who had decided that he did not want to be one anymore, and was trying to clear out. The others in his group shot him in the leg just in case he was an enemy - Viet Cong - in disguise. No one trusted anyone.

As the weeks went by it was evident with all the towns falling to the enemy advance that the South could not hold out much longer. People began to prepare for escape in various ways and those in charge of the orphanages were anxious to find somewhere for safety for the childrcn. Thcy knew that food and care would be nil for most of these children once the country fell. Plane loads of babies and children were being organised with foreign countries. America,

Australia and England in particular were sending in special flights to help in evacuation.

Our own small orphanage also had babies and children, sixteen in all. Then there were our own three tribal babies, Peter, Paul and Mary, whom we would never have been able to reunite with their families at that stage. We started to look around for help. Because we did not want to lose them to another country and New Zealand was keeping a low profile I approached Rosemary Taylor, a well known Australian running an orphanage in Saigon, and asked if she would allow 'our babies' on Australia's airlift. She kindly agreed if we could have the children in a certain building ready to leave for the airport at a certain time. We will always be grateful to her. I went back to the Sisters, packed up clothing and necessities, and set out in our trusty van for Saigon. When we arrived, there were babies everywhere, all over the floor and anywhere a baby could fit in! At some stage we got the signal to move - that meant bundling babies into vehicles in shoe boxes or anything which could be used as a bassinet.

We moved away in convoy, and as I was driving along my dread was that I would be held up and lose touch and be refused entry to the airport. This did not happen but at one stage we had to 'abandon ship' and all board buses for the last leg to the flights standing by. Before we could move an official went down his list of names and numbers, warning us that if we were one over the number we would not get permission to go any further.

At last we could stop holding our breath! The bus began to move and we arrived on the tarmac beside a large 747. Sr. Dorothy had agreed to accompany the children to Australia and the authorities were grateful for more hands to cope with feeding, changing etc. throughout the flight. I was more than grateful that she would be able to ensure that 'our three' would not be 'lost' in Australia but be able to travel on to New Zealand.

All the babies were labelled with the names of the home they had come from. Orphanage workers and drivers, besides people like myself, set to work quickly helping to load the precious live cargo. The small babies were easiest but there were many older children, four- to ten-year-olds, who put up great resistance to being forced into this 'big black hole'. The poor little kids must have been terrified and I wonder how many of them still suffer from the results of this trauma.

At last the doors were closed and the plane ready to taxi out. We moved back to wave to them, thankful that they were flying off to freedom.

While we were busy loading up this Australian flight another load was being prepared for America. That big plane had moved out on to the runway ahead of ours. It took off as ours prepared to follow. Suddenly I heard someone close by cry out "Look!" pointing to the American flight. It was not gaining height as we expected but flying lower and lower towards Bien Hoa. We stood there in utter shock. Was this sabotage? was the first thought that came to our minds.

That evening we learned details of the tragedy. The plane we saw leaving was a jumbo jet with two floors, lower and upper. The older children were in the top compartment with carers, most of whom were volunteers, while the babies were on the lower floor. Once the pilot was aware of a problem he had turned the plane to try to land at the military base at Bien Hoa, but he could not reach it and the plane came down in a rice field. All the babies on the bottom floor had been killed together with their carers, while those on the top survived. My great friend, Dr. Merritt Stark, was on the top level while his daughter Laurie, whom I knew well and had seen a few days before, was killed with all those on the lower deck. May they all rest in peace! The shock of all that tragedy left us completely stunned for long afterwards. After some days we learnt the reason

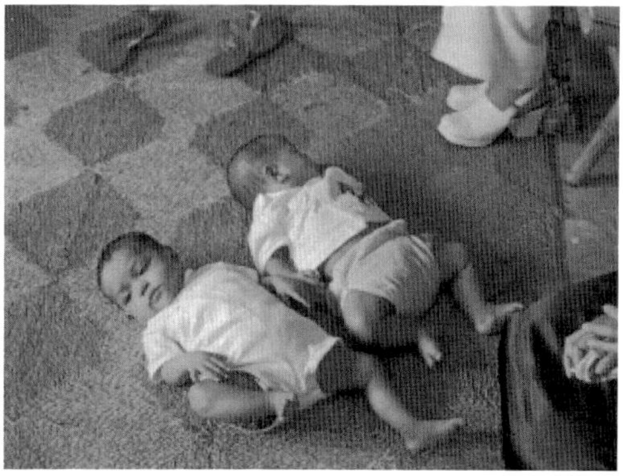

Peter and Paul

Sister Dorothy with Peter, Paul and Mary boarding the flight to Australia. Nhet could not accompany them any further.

Babies and children brought together at the Australian Embassy awaiting transportation - destination unknown.

for the catastrophe: a damaged rear door had not closed properly and so the plane could not stay airborne.

Many years later, in 1992, I went out to visit the site of the crash. All that is left there now is a part of the fuselage stuck firmly in the mud, with incense sticks burning on it continuously. Some of the locals claim to hear the crying of babies each night.

By this time a feeling of foreboding had swept over the whole country and one could feel the panic taking over. The New Zealand Embassy staff were still working and I would drop in as often as I could to check proceedings with them. One day when I was on my motor bike I found that the bridge over which I usually travelled had been blocked off, so I turned and found another way. It wasn't until I reached the Embassy and they greeted me with "How did you get here?" that I learnt of the attack on the Palace by one of "our" planes. The pilot apparently had had orders to bomb the part of the country in which he had lived and where his family still lived. It was too much to expect of him. His next best target was the Palace close by!

I carried on with serious things that needed doing and with work at the camps, all the time wondering just what was going to happen, and when.

One Sunday morning for no particular reason I called in to the Embassy again and was confronted with a proposition: a Hercules would be leaving that afternoon on its way to New Zealand and I was strongly advised to go with it. I had no intention of leaving at that time but I was anxious to find a way of getting M. Lea out of the country, if possible, and if she wanted to go rather than have to face possible imprisonment again. I hurried back to the convent where I put the offer to Sister. She had so little time to make up her mind on such a decision but she agreed to come with me. My plan was to fly with her to Singapore where she would connect with a flight to New Zealand; I would return to Saigon any way I could find. We went into the airport in an Embassy car and drove straight out to the tarmac where the Hercules was waiting. We had not gone through any departure procedure or immigration counter but were not too worried at that stage. There were other New Zealanders on the flight with us and we duly landed in Singapore to be told that we would stay there the night and travel on the next day.

We were driven to a beautiful hotel and given a room the like of which we had never seen before. The only problem was that neither of us had any foreign money with which to pay for it. What to do? Then I had a brainwave and contacted the New Zealand Embassy who kindly agreed to pay the account for us; our Sisters would reimburse them in Wellington.

That afternoon when everyone was congregated in the foyer of the hotel awaiting the bus to take them all back to the airport one of the New Zealand Embassy staff arrived with an important message for me. He assured me that I should not try to go back as Saigon had almost fallen. Another split-second decision! What to do? I boarded the Hercules again with M. Lea. Making ourselves as comfortable as possible on the canvas seats running down both sides of the plane, we set off on one of the coldest flights I have ever known! After what seemed a very long time we landed in Darwin, Australia, at midnight their time. In spite of the terrible storms and floods they were having at that time, the locals took time to provide us with a hot meal, so welcome, and armed us with blankets to warm us on the rest of the trip. The next day we landed at Whenuapai, the Air Force base out of Auckland, where we were again fed with the most delicious Sunday roast dinner. I contacted our Sisters by phone to tell them where we were, as none of them had known our plans, and waited for them to pick us up. One small baby had accompanied us on the flight, destined for her foster parents who were at the airport to meet her. How relieved they were to welcome a new member to the family safe and sound!

Accompanied by two New Zealand servicewomen Sr. M. Laurence (third from left) with Sr. M. Lea (second from left) leave the aircraft at Auckland having fled the unrest in Vietnam together with the first Vietnamese orphan to arrive in New Zealand.

Eventually we were picked up and arrived home with the Sisters at our convent in Auckland. Of course Sr. M. Lea had never been to New Zealand before but she was a great 'hit' and soon developed a great affection for our Sisters and for New Zealand.

There were so many things that I still needed to do! I contacted our General Council in Rome to let them know what had been happening in Vietnam, as we had been unable to make contact with anyone from Saigon immediately before we left. I was particularly concerned for three Sisters who had had a harrowing time escaping from North Vietnam in 1954 when the Communists had first taken over and were now living in Saigon. I asked my superiors for permission to go back to try to get them out. I had no idea how I might be able to do that but I was willing to try. Thankfully they gave me the 'go-ahead' and I looked for a flight to Vietnam, leaving the following Sunday. I had been home just a week.

I flew out of Auckland via Singapore where I stayed overnight with the Sisters of the Good Shepherd RGS. An old friend, Tony Bradley, another New Zealander, was also going back to try to get some of his friends out, as well as an American living in New Zealand, a Mr Thompson, who wanted to get his in-laws out. So there were three of us, and I did appreciate the support from those two good men. The next morning we were back at the airport in Singapore thinking that we would have little trouble in boarding a flight to Vietnam. To our surprise we found that crowds of people, some of them waiting for days, had been trying to go back in to Saigon to help people out. How would we ever get any further?

At last I reached the counter and the girl examined my passport and papers. Then she told me what I didn't want to hear, the flight was full. "But go and wait!" she added. I felt strangely confident. If I was destined to return it would happen, and if not, there was nothing more I could do.

Just before the flight was to take off the girl called me again and said "Go!" I didn't need a second invitation. I began to breathe again only when I strapped myself into my seat . So we took off for Saigon. My problems were not over yet, of course.

How was I going to go in through customs? My passport had not been stamped to show that I had left? Tony came to my rescue. He offered to take my small bag with him while I made for the VIP lounge. I barged straight through to the outside of the terminal under the surprised eyes of some Canadian personnel, who were awaiting their flight out of Saigon. No-one stopped me to ask why I was there, and I met Tony outside when he managed to get through. I collected my bag and arranged to meet later in the week at the Embassy.

Once out on the street I could feel the change in atmosphere from the week before. The streets were almost deserted and there was an eerie silence over all. I found a little Lambretta with one or two other passengers on it which took me out to Thu Duc where I was dropped off at the turnoff. The walk from there was about 20-30 minutes and I was glad when I saw the double gates of the convent compound looming up. Alas! Those gates were firmly locked, and not a soul in sight to open them! There was a back gate that I knew of, but that was locked too. There was nothing left to do but to scramble through the barbed wire that surrounded everyone's property in those days.

After trying a few locked doors with no success I found one that had been missed and I entered the convent unbeknown to anyone. The house was so quiet I guessed where the Sisters would be and made my way upstairs to the chapel. Sure enough, they all were at evening prayer. They could not believe their eyes! I was supposed to be safely in New Zealand! After another 'welcome back' I could see the fear and hopelessness in their faces as they awaited their fate. That night most of them spent the night huddled under tables on the ground floor while explosions and gunfire continued outside. I was too tired to care at that stage and stayed in my bed on the top floor trying to get some sleep.

That evening Mr Thompson watched from the roof of his hotel in Saigon as the airport was attacked and planes were blown up.

The next morning I suggested to the three Sisters who were willing to leave the country that we should go to our convent in Saigon before all the roads were cut. We set out promptly in our small French Peugeot with me at the wheel. We soon found that my fears

American Embassy - on stand-by

People kept arriving all afternoon

A Chinook lands to transfer people to the air craft carriers

Inching around the swimming pool

Mr Thompson with some of his dependants

were well-grounded, the main highway into the city was already cut off. We went the long way round by the back route, and after about two hours we reached our destination. The three Sisters stayed at the convent while I went on into town to try to find a way out of the chaos. I spent all that day going from one office to another to request four seats on anything still leaving. Absolutely nothing! All that was available was already spoken for by employees of the Americans and their families. Why should we be considered? I went home that evening resigned to whatever would be our fate.

During the night another offensive took place, this time very close. There was a military base not far away and that was the target. We, all the Sisters and our dependants, spent the night huddled together under the stairs praying ceaselessly. Our prayers were heard and we all emerged in the morning unexpectedly! News over the radio warned people of a curfew. No one should be out on the streets unless needed at their jobs. After unsuccessfully telephoning people I knew, I decided that the only way to find out what was going on was to go and see for myself.

I took off on foot up the main road where the only thing visible was a motor bike coming my way. I stopped it and asked for a ride up to the corner where I could walk down to the New Zealand Embassy building. I don't know what I expected to find there as I already knew that the New Zealand staff had left, but I carried on in hope. Sure enough when I arrived two of the Vietnamese staff were already there, including one of the girls who worked the Telex machine. The two of us sent direct messages to Wellington telling them of the situation and requesting their help, though I knew there was nothing anyone there could do at that stage.

During that morning (April 29th) Mr. Thompson arrived at the Embassy with his in-laws. The only one missing then was Tony and who would know where to start looking for him? I rang the Sisters and asked them to find a vehicle to bring our three Sisters to the Embassy at once, and they duly arrived. What we were actually going to do we did not know. We could only take one moment at a time. I didn't want to leave without Tony so in desperation I began to look for keys for the Embassy cars parked in the driveway. After forcing some drawers in the offices upstairs we found a set of keys that fitted and after connecting the battery set out to find our missing friend. Looking for a needle in a haystack was nothing compared to our search! Time was moving on. We had to give up and return to the Embassy where everyone was waiting. (Tony did not return in time to escape with us. He was held for some months by the Communist authorities but finally returned safely to New Zealand.)

During all that time panic had really set in. Desperate people were making for the harbour to board anything that would float. Others were congregated outside the fence of the American Embassy. Some tried scaling the walls and were knocked off by the rifles of the soldiers there to keep guard. At some stage a French man arrived from nowhere and offered to drive us all up to the American compound in the hope that through the company of Mr. Thompson, an American, we could gain entrance. (Actually, Mr. Thompson and his dependants could have been gone early that day but he refused to move until he knew we would be all right. I will always be grateful to him for his kindness and concern).

There was chaos all around the American Embassy, with soldiers smashing windscreens of any cars that got up too close and warning people to keep back. That did not have a lot of effect. By the time we had driven around the block once we could see the hopelessness of it. We all got out of the car and pushed our way through the crowds, following Mr. Thompson who was tall and powerfully built. The guard on the gate saw that he was the nearest thing to an American, and waved us all through. While I was more than relieved to be inside, I felt for all those poor people now abandoned to their fate.

Many of them had been promised protection for being employees of the Americans. For the rest of that day, we shuffled our way slowly around the yard. At one stage we noticed a dark line in the sky. It was a fleet of Chinooks going to different parts of the city to collect people from pre-arranged pick-up points.

We spent all afternoon inching our way around the swimming pool towards a small gate which led into the main Embassy building. A gap between the two was the only space on the ground where a Chinook could land, after trees had been cut down. As evening drew on we wondered what hope there still was. By 8.00 p.m. our group was at the head of the line waiting, waiting, waiting for the next landing. And then it happened! A Chinook came over and settled. It could only just fit into the space at the back of the Embassy. Once the gate was unlocked we made a beeline for the aircraft and scrambled aboard. I just can't imagine how many people were there gazing up at us as we took off into a dark sky. Red tracer bullets were flying around us, fired from different directions of the city, hoping to bring us down.

As we rose above the chaos a young Vietnamese mother with a baby in arms became hysterical. She had just realised that her little boy of four years had not followed her on to the plane. He must have been parted from her by the crush of the crowd between the gate and the aircraft. Acutely distressed for her, we tried to encourage her to expect him on the next flight, and we prayed and prayed that he would turn up.

Almost before we knew it we had arrived out in the South China Sea and had landed on the deck of an American aircraft carrier. (Its name was well known but I have forgotten it now. This whole time is a blur of noise and hurry and crowds and fear in my memory). Once we disembarked we were shown down into the bowels of the ship and waited in lines to be checked, named and tagged with hospital name tags together with numbers. I offered to carry a frail elderly man's bag which seemed too heavy for him and gave him mine to be checked through. We both laughed, wondering what the officials thought of the mismatched contents. I cannot remember where we waited after that, but I did have time to write notes to my mother and the Sisters in New Zealand to tell them where we were.

Letter To Mum:

> *29th April*
>
> *Approximately 10pm*
>
> *…I am sitting on the floor of a huge aircraft carrier with 378 other refugees. We have just been flown out from Saigon by helicopter, 8 p.m., and are due to be transferred to a troop carrier in about two hours. We will be aboard her for about five days until we reach Guam…*

A sailor on the ship offered to post my mail for me, which he duly did, with a distinctive envelope and postal stamp (which years later I found at home when going through my mother's old correspondence.)

At approximately 2.00 a.m. a group of us were loaded into a small boat about the size of a large dinghy and to my surprise sailed out of the end of the ship. (I have never worked out how we managed to find our way out to the water). We arrived at length at a platform to which was attached a rope ladder, which in turn was hanging from the side of a large cargo ship called "The Greenport". Nothing was clearly visible at that time of night, and maybe just as well. Some of us might not have dared to risk falling off the platform as it rocked from side to side in the rough sea. The exercise now was to catch the end of the rope ladder at the right moment and scale the ladder with one hand while the other tried to cling to a small bag of possessions. I could not understand how mothers and babies managed to do

Orders finally came from Washington for everyone to be picked up.

An aircraft carrier launch ferries people to the Greenport

All unnecessary baggage was left behind

Fishing boat passengers hoping to be picked up

On the deck of the Greenport bound for Subic Bay in the Philippines.

The deck of the Greenport

Making the most of the sea cruise

The only toilet facilities on board!

that, but in desperation almost anything is possible. We were lucky enough to be some of the first refugees to board so we had the choice of where we could camp on the deck. In daylight we found that the decking was cast iron and hot enough to roast us all alive when the sun shone on it all day.

There were two or three holds which as time went on became crammed with people who could no longer fit on to the deck. How they didn't suffocate down there I never knew.

The young Vietnamese mother who had lost her four-year-old stayed close to us all the time. Alas! there was no sign of the little boy, and I wept with her in her anguish. This young mother was going to join her husband who was already in America, waiting and hoping for her safe arrival.

We sat out at sea without moving anywhere for maybe two days in the boiling heat. The only food was small tins of "C" rations used by the army and well out of date, but we were hardly in any situation to complain and received them with gratitude. More and more people joined us and the deck began to fill up quickly. Water for drinking was rationed and we would line up every morning to get our quota for the day. There were no showers or washing facilities unless one wanted to stand under a pressure-hose firing out sea-water! I didn't fancy that too much. Toilets had been erected down the sides of the ship, partitioned off with sacking if I remember rightly.

As I gazed out and towards Vietnam one morning I wondered if the sun had got to me. The horizon seemed to be a line of white – what on earth was it? As the day drew on the white line came closer and we could see a whole fleet of small fishing boats coming towards us, many flying Red Cross flags. They circled around the ship and it seemed to our consternation that the crew were going to do nothing about picking up these people. After what seemed to us a very long time, the ladder was thrown over and more people came aboard, abandoning their boats. We learnt later that the captain had had to wait for orders before he could take the "boat people" aboard. The ship by now was close to packed and the motors started up. We began to move, where to, I did not know. Some of the men who had left their wives and families behind and had had time to think about it, wanted to go back, but now there was no hope of doing that unless they were prepared to swim! It was sad to see their dilemma.

The crew were very vigilant, on watch constantly for any fighting breaking out, and they would fire their pistols into the air to bring situations under control when needed. The days were long and hot with little space in which to move. Babies were in need of milk so I spent time tracking down milk powder, delivering it to the mothers, returning lost children to their families and just being there for anyone who wanted anything. Each day our clothes collected more

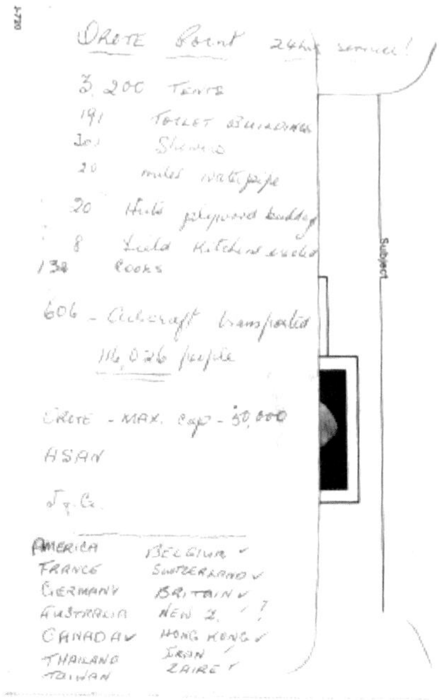

Orete Point 24hrs service!

3,200 Tents
191 Toilet buildings
30? Showers
20 miles water pipe
20 Huts plywood buildings
8 field kitchens ...
134 cooks

606 - Aircraft transported
114,026 people

Orete - Max. cap - 50,000
ASAN
J.g.C.

America — Belgium ✓
France — Switzerland ✓
Germany — Britain ✓
Australia — New Z. ?
Canada ✓ — Hong Kong ✓
Thailand — Iran
Taiwan — Zaire ✓

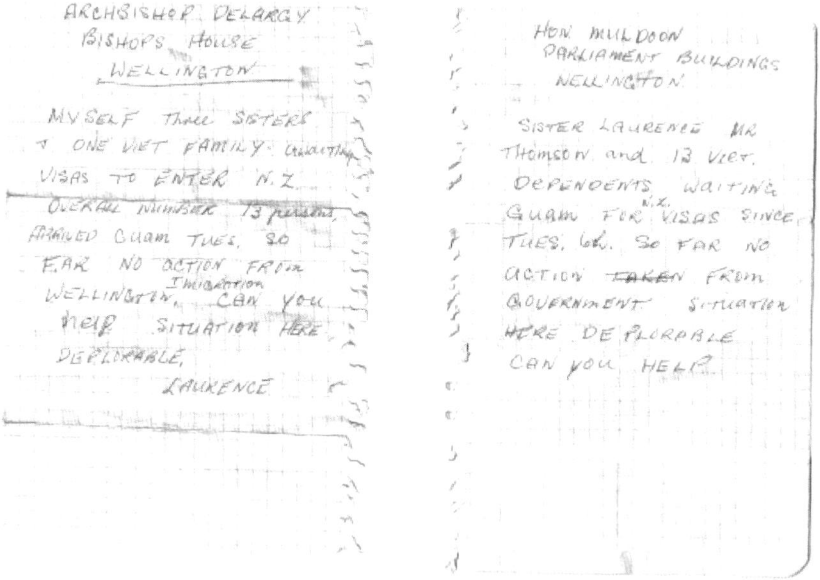

ARCHBISHOP DELARGY
BISHOPS HOUSE
WELLINGTON

MYSELF THREE SISTERS + ONE VIET FAMILY awaiting VISAS TO ENTER N.Z. OVERALL NUMBER 13 persons. ARRIVED Guam TUES. SO FAR NO ACTION FROM WELLINGTON IMMIGRATION. CAN YOU help SITUATION HERE DEPLORABLE.
LAURENCE

HON. MULDOON
PARLIAMENT BUILDINGS
WELLINGTON

SISTER LAURENCE MR THOMSON and 13 VIET. DEPENDENTS WAITING GUAM FOR N.Z. VISAS SINCE TUES. 6th. SO FAR NO ACTION ~~TAKEN~~ FROM GOVERNMENT. SITUATION HERE DEPLORABLE CAN YOU HELP.

Copies of the draft letters from my notebook

salt from the sea spray until they became as stiff as if they had been starched. One night at midnight I took refuge in one of the toilets and changed my clothes, taking great delight in throwing the disgusting soiled things overboard.

I don't know how long it was before we sailed into Subic Bay where Third Nationals (people who were leaving their native land for another) were allowed to go ashore for a short time. Our real destination, we learned, was Guam. I went ashore to see if I could contact any New Zealand Embassy personnel but when I saw the futility of that I asked for a case of apples to take back to the ship as a change from cold "C" rations. This was handed over without any trouble, for which I was very grateful. We returned to the ship for the next leg of the "cruise" but on boarding we were told that all Third Nationals and their dependants were to be transported from Subic Bay to Guam by military flight. I was very sorry to say goodbye to all our friends on board but pleased I could leave them the case of apples. We met up later in Guam.

We left Subic Bay on a cargo flight, no seats, and sitting in four lines the full length of the plane. The huge cargo belts were strung over us and hooked onto the end of the line; that was all the support we had. The people who managed to sit at the sides with backs supported were those with "first class" accommodation compared to the rest of us sitting on the floor in two lines with nothing to lean against. I have no idea how long the flight took but it seemed forever before we landed and boarded buses which took us out to the Orote Point "tent city".

Life In Guam

The buses deposited us beside a large hangar with real mattresses spread on the ground. We did not ask what they were for before we made use of the sheer luxury, we fell on them and stretched out. Once again we were checked, tagged and numbered; then we were

An aerial view of Tent City - Guam. Army tents in rows.

shown huge army tents being set up as accommodation and we were furnished with stretcher-beds. One tent was allotted to maybe twenty people. Ours served as 'home' all the time we were there trying to find a country that would accept our three Sisters.

At the very first opportunity I went with Mai, the distraught Vietnamese mother, to see if a message could be put over the loud-speaker system asking if anyone had found a little boy. Imagine our joy when a reply came: "Yes! Yes!" Some soldiers had found the lost four-year-old and had taken good care of him, intending to adopt him if nobody claimed him. Mother and son were soon reunited and this time we all cried for joy and relief.

I can't remember what the water situation was like in the camp but there were portable toilets set up. We stood in queues for hours to collect meals and maybe drinking water at the same time. There were no shower facilities but over the months I had become almost used to that.

Representatives from different countries set up a process through which the people could apply to go to a country of their choice as long as they had feasible identification. Alas! New Zealand was conspicuous by its absence. The only channel left for the Sisters was to make application to France since we RNDMs were originally a French order and still had sisters in France who would take responsibility for the three refugees.

While we were waiting for the paperwork to be completed I tried to find a New Zealand Consulate or Embassy through which I could make contact with family and sisters in New Zealand who yet again had no idea where I was. The only contact I could find was through the Red Cross who said that they had a New Zealander belonging to them. At that stage I thought that they were giving me contact with an office or some official body, but to my delight the contact was a wonderful New Zealander living on Guam with her husband, who came to find me at once. They opened their home to us. (Margaret Poole has remained a wonderful friend to this day. Her husband Fred has since died and Margaret has returned to live in New Zealand. I always think of them with great affection and gratitude for accepting us with such warm and loving hospitality). Actually it was in their home that the four of us were able at last to have a shower and wash our clothes. I hate to think what we must have looked like on arrival. After our first rendezvous with the Pooles, we were picked up on our return to the camp and told in no uncertain terms that no one was allowed to leave the

Fred and Margaret Poole on their front lawn

camp without permission. Lucky we hadn't known that before our outing!

On the 'Greenport', a very old cargo ship, a German girl had given me what aid money she still had left for refugees, so I had a little cash to help out when needed. A women's organisation on Guam opened a stall to distribute clothing to the people. I helped there during the days while we were waiting to see what and where our next move would be. I was planning to return home once the Sisters were fixed up but again I was stuck without transport and with no money to buy a ticket.

Again the Pooles' came to our rescue. I was able to contact our Sisters in Auckland by phone. They were wondering why I wasn't home yet! Through a travel agency they sent me a ticket for whenever I would need it.

We spent almost two weeks in 'Tent City' and each day more and more people were arriving, telling of different ways they had escaped, and worrying about where they could go to from here, and how their loved ones left behind were faring.

At last our three Vietnamese Sisters received their papers giving them entry to France and the correct exit papers from Guam. Since we were now officially on our way we were moved to another location to await transport. The new 'housing' was right beside the sea in what had been army barracks. We took up residence, back on the floor, in a large room which accommodated a great number of refugees awaiting departure to many parts of the world. After a few days there, and satisfied that the Sisters were fully prepared to reach their destination in France, I said goodbye to them and made my way to the commercial airport. There I said goodbye to our wonderful friends the Pooles and boarded a 'normal' flight with seats and attendants. I was on my way home - May 1975.

Tent City

In the camp

Mr Thompson in Tent City

Taking showers - open air!

The "departure lounge" where we rested while waiting to leave Guam

Asan where we were moved to from Tent City. No stretchers here!

My three dependants before leaving for France.

PART 2

Chapter 7

Return To Vietnam 1992 - 2003

After the evacuation of 1975 I had never imagined myself going back to Vietnam. For fourteen years I was busy in Samoa.

One day in 1991 when I was working back in New Zealand my attention was caught by a newspaper advertisement. Volunteers were wanted for VSA (Voluntary Service Abroad), it said, to assist in the New Zealand Government development project in the Central Province of Qui Nhon, Vietnam. Among the skills required they particularly wanted English Language Teaching for a High School and for a Teachers' Training College. At that time I was assisting with English teaching at the Mangere Immigration Centre.

Why not? I thought. Why not apply? If I can do it here, why not there? So I sent in my application. To my surprise I was accepted. With the blessing of our provincial leaders I, with four other New Zealand volunteers, began to make ready.

Vietnamese language preparations took place at the Mangere Centre where we were grateful for a Vietnamese language expert to teach us. I tried hard to recall and revise words and tones I had long forgotten. My earlier experience in Vietnam had never made me fluent in Vietnamese anyway. In all my years at Phuoc Long I had normally spoken the Montagnard language which is totally unrelated to Vietnamese. Being a tonal language Vietnamese is doubly hard for a Kiwi to learn. Beginners can make so many blunders which give great amusement to the native speakers.

By February 1992 we were as ready as we would ever be for take-off. We left Auckland bound for a stop-over at Singapore, flying into Saigon, no, Ho Chi Minh City now, the following day. I had mixed feelings, wondering what I would encounter, visualizing the place as I had left it seventeen years before.

On our arrival I could see that not a lot had changed. The Spitfire hangars were still there close to the runways where American pilots had taken off to attack jungle areas where enemy soldiers were supposed to be in hiding. In the arrival terminal things seemed even more chaotic than they had been years before. We had to scramble over bags littering the floor where they had been thrown by the baggage handlers, in the hopes that we might be lucky enough to find our own. After what seemed hours we eventually passed through Immigration, the only bit of order prevailing, it seemed. Everything felt unfriendly, scrutinizing, suspicious.

We were met by a group from the Qui Nhon Red Cross who were to take responsibility for us while we were working there. They took us in a Red Cross vehicle to a small motel where we were given accommodation of a kind that night. Somehow our Sisters had learnt of my return and the place where we would be staying that evening, and several of them arrived on their motorbikes! What a wonderful reunion that was! Even better, they offered to take me to the convent to meet with the other Sisters there. It was an unforgettable meeting with Sisters whom I had not seen for over seventeen years.

Saigon/Ho Chi Minh City still had the large population I could remember but there were very few cars or motorbikes. Mostly push bikes were being used due to petrol shortages and costs. The absence of barbed wire and manned military lookouts on bridges was one obvious improvement. I had last seen the city in the throes of war.

Saigon as I had known it was gone. It had lost its vibrance and life and its flashes of affluence. The military presence was gone, the police were inconspicuous, the buildings were drab.

The next day we set out for Qui Nhon in the Red Cross van, a trip of about ten to twelve hours. We were warned at the outset that cameras could not be used for recording anything we saw on the way as the Government at that time was strict about conditions within the country being known outside.

The poverty in the countryside was very evident as we journeyed through the various villages. I had been in Qui Nhon once before, when Dorothy and I had been invited to stay with the New Zealand Medical Team after we had been released from the prison camp in 1975. We had enjoyed that weekend with those wonderful New Zealanders who had kept the local hospital running and were thought so highly of by the people, North and South alike. Now I could not even remember where we had stayed or recognise the town at all.

On our arrival this time we were billeted in the Government-run hotel, by no means five-star, but adequate for the tired state we were all in. The heat and the distance we had travelled both contributed to our weariness.

There was no form of communication and the only way we could let home or VSA Wellington know that we had arrived safely was through fax from the local Post Office.

QUI NHON - FAX

To: Clare Murphy
PO Box 30 575
LOWER HUTT
NEW ZEALAND
(04) 5663 042 Fax: 64 4 566 8328

From: Sheila O'Toole
PO Box 12
Qui Nhon
VIETNAM
Fax: 54 56 22444

Dear Clare and all my Sisters,

I had hoped to have a letter off to you long ago but since our arrival here we have had little time to ourselves. Yesterday we started six weeks' language course so after that we will have a routine of work which will be good. We arrived in H.C.M. city about 9 p.m. in the evening and were met by the Red Cross Team who gave us a great welcome and took us to the hotel. Some of my friends had been at the Airport earlier but because we were late arriving they had gone home. We were in H.C.M. city for five days and after three attempts my friends found me out and took me to their house where we had a few hours of hilarity!! It was great! From the moment I stepped off the plane I felt I had never been away and I slipped back into the culture so naturally. The language has come naturally alive – "His promise…"

Our journey from Saigon to Qui Nhon took about 15 hours but it was most interesting and we all enjoyed it. The preparations for the Tet - New Year - were in full swing when we got here so it was a very good time to come. With special Tet food, fire crackers and general revelry we were truly spoilt by the Vietnamese hospitality. We have been introduced to all the special committees with whom we will be working. They have all been friendly and welcoming, and the people in the streets also!

Hope all the Regional Days go well - with you in spirit and prayer. Missing Community! Forgot to tell you before I left that there is plenty of room between the lines - of the papers I left. The address above is enough.

Love and prayers, Sheila

The following morning we were taken to be introduced to "our house" which had once been the property of the doctor in charge of the hospital. It had later been used as a kindergarten before being cleaned up and prepared for our arrival. In the main house there were two bedrooms, one large living room, a dining room, a toilet and shower combined, and a storage space at the back. Outside the back door there were three other small rooms plus a toilet, shower and kitchen. A high concrete wall surrounded us with a strong double iron gate, locked on the inside, to keep us in? Or to keep others out?

A sandy space between the front of the house and the wall was a wilderness where later a couple of us worked in our spare time and managed to transform it into a fairly acceptable garden.

A woman had already been employed to be the general housekeeper, cook as well as an interpreter.

Qui Nhon was situated beside the sea somewhat off the beaten track. Anywhere else and in normal conditions it would be considered a perfect holiday resort, but not here; here the beach is the town's public toilets and no one would venture near it for any other purpose. Further around the shore there was a private hotel where the beach area was reserved for the guests; we could frequent that if we wanted to.

The square in the centre of the town, I was told, was where enemy soldiers who had been captured were taken out and shot. I could well imagine it.

Everyone seemed to be working seven days a week so we let it be known from the outset that we functioned only five days a week, in true Kiwi fashion! Within the first few days we met with the Province People's Committee and the Province Leader who officially welcomed us, and later we were taken to meet the groups with whom each team member was assigned to work. The Water Engineer and the District Nurse were assigned to a coastal village to assist in water installation and health on the Village level; the maintenance worker was assigned to the Province Hospital; the other teacher went to the Teachers' Training College for English, and I was allotted to the High School.

My job was with the gifted students, all high stream learners who were chosen from all the District Schools in the Province. I did enjoy my time there and have been gratified since to see many of the pupils getting good positions in Saigon or now running their own businesses.

Because we were the first foreigners to take up residence since 1975 the authorities were very suspicious of us on the one hand, and extremely protective on the other. They were genuinely concerned that some of the people who had suffered much at the hands of invading foreigners during the war would look on us as enemy and try to vent their anger one way or another. On the whole we saw little or no sign of this except on one occasion: two of us were riding our bicycles down the road when we saw a cycle heading for us from the other side of the road. At first we thought the young rider wanted to get to our side so we tried to make a space for him. When he kept trying to drive his cycle into us we realized just what he was on about, and put some distance between us.

Many of the ordinary people could not believe that we could be there solely to help them without expecting to get something out of it for ourselves. Our movements were very restricted and we were advised strongly not to open the gate to anyone we did not know personally, without getting permission from the authorities first.

Outside our locked gate was a power pole with a loud-speaker attached. Every morning at approximately 5.00 a.m. this loud-speaker would blare out deafening music and all the news and laws to abide by that day, principally for the benefit of the market stall holders across the road. This proved more than a frustration to some members of the Team but no matter how many times I complained to the authorities about it, nothing changed. I could understand their thinking: we were in their country to help them to make the changes they wanted, and that wasn't one of them.

Being named the 'Team Leader', every Saturday morning I had to meet with those responsible for us to report on what each Team Member had done the previous week, what they planned to do for the following week, and where they would go. This all proved very exasperating for those volunteers, all professionals in their jobs, who had come from a country like New Zealand where only normal restrictions existed, like driving on the correct side of the road. However we gradually worked through these frustrations and those with whom we worked closely began to appreciate what each one was endeavouring to do with and for the Project.

My associates at the school were very kind, though understandably they kept their distance to avoid the suspicion of the police, who would always want to know exactly what we had been talking about.

There seemed to be no classroom as such for my English classes so I was allocated a small space next to the school tuck shop. You can imagine what a source of perpetual distraction to the students that was, and what a major hindrance to their listening skills, to say nothing of the frustration for their teacher. After a period of perhaps four months' endurance I felt it time to submit my problem to the Principal for the sake of the students as well as my own.

It took a few months more before a regular classroom was made available. Even then the only equipment in the room was really antiquated desks into each of which three or four students crammed. With assistance from VSA and a local carpenter who became one of my firm friends, we installed blackboards and pin-up panels. By the end of almost three years this room was finally equipped with single desks and chairs, a novelty to students within this prestigious school, and we also had library books, listening equipment and other learning aids.

It was evident that education had been neglected for many years especially here in this central part of the country, which had been a strong centre of support for the Communist invasion of the South. The students I had were the cream of all the schools in the Province; they were keen and intelligent and learned very quickly. In the local culture a teacher was someone to look up to and respect so I never had the slightest behavioural problem.

I was always careful about my subject matter and my casual comments, as I knew that whatever I said in the classroom would be reported back to those in authority by the students whose job it was to monitor me. I was very much aware that wherever I was, teaching or with a group of people socially, there would be one or two people there just to record my conversation or subject input. Two subjects I especially avoided like a plague were politics and religion and I was always careful never to be drawn into discussion on these subjects.

A group of my students at Quoe Hoc High School

One of the evening classes at the Red Cross.

Bac Si Bong and a group from the Red Cross.

Besides spending two to three hours each day with students in the school, some of the Team were asked if we would help with evening classes for adults at a Language Centre run by the Red Cross. At that time the Vietnamese Red Cross were not recognised internationally and we were fully aware that the title did not guarantee that the funds collected from students went in the right direction. That, however, was not our problem. We were concerned only that the students received value for their money. The driving force to learn was so strong that all of those in the classes came after a long, hard day's work; they really needed to go home and relax rather than move into another situation of high concentration. In those days they also learned very little with immediate relevance to their work, if they were employed, and it was difficult for them to find the fees to keep coming. What drove many of them was the fact that if they could master English they would be able to get better paying jobs in the future.

The day on which we were preparing topics - speaking for the examination (June 9th 1996).

A Kiwi growing in our front garden.

I enjoyed my time with all the students.

Once they knew English-speaking teachers were available the class attendance grew. At one stage I was faced with trying to teach one hundred students speaking and listening skills and I soon saw the futility of that. It was a good opportunity to get to know the wider community though, and I still remember so many of them with affection.

During one of our evening classes when we were working on an exercise about "going on a holiday", I asked the class who could tell us about a holiday they had had. Not one student ventured to raise a hand. On probing more I was astonished to learn that no one in the class, all adults, had ever been anywhere but where they lived. They had no idea what a holiday was! Their lives were geared to work, work, work, and to making ends meet.

Church and Religion

Before I arrived I had wondered what my position would be with regard to the local Church. Would I be able to attend Mass, meet the priests, speak to the local Sisters? To my surprise I learned that the local newspaper had had an article about the arrival of a New Zealand Team including a Catholic Sister! A ploy to bring Church and State together on more friendly terms?

Actually to this day religious liberty in Vietnam is something of a myth. An attempt at government nationalisation of the Church was a miserable failure. A crowd can go to Mass on Sunday and openly pour out on to the street from the church door. This 'proves' that there is freedom of religion, but people who convert to Christianity face subtle persecution, discrimination at work, job loss, petty and damaging government surveillance, hindrance to or deprivation of education for their children.

Church involvement among the ethnic minorities is particularly unacceptable, being seen as a potential source of disaffection and even of active protest among the under-privileged and poverty-stricken. Without any warning police raid the homes of people only suspected of doubtful loyalty and terrorise them by brutal beatings and threats of worse penalties. From the Hmong, the tribes of the Chinese border areas, hundreds have been imprisoned in forced-labour camps. At all times I had to be discreet without appearing to act suspiciously.

With the help of our interpreter I found the local Catholic church not far by bicycle from where we were billeted. The hours of Mass on week days, however, were somewhat early, 5.00 a.m. - 5.30 a.m. This practice came about throughout the country when the Government required all the people to be out at the crack of dawn for their ritual of communal exercises before reporting for their assigned communal works. If any people wanted to attend Mass, as most practising

Catholics did, it had to be before the controlled day began, hence the early prayers, which to this day is still the custom.

Accompanied by our 'minders' on another occasion, I met with the priest and the Bishop. They lived in a huge building, formerly the seminary, but very much empty of young men studying for the priesthood at that stage. The Bishop had his residence in another part of that huge compound which must have been beautiful in its day.

Close by there was a community of Sisters called 'Lovers of the Cross' who ran a kindergarten. That permission had not long been granted by the Government. Prior to that, Religious Sisters were forbidden to engage in any works for the people and the schools and hospitals they ran up to 1975 were all confiscated and belonged to the State. One would wonder how the Sisters had lived and survived at all.

I soon made friends with them and they were delighted to meet up with a fellow Religious from "outside". Before long I was assisting them and a handful of novices with learning English. The Sisters were very kind to me but for their own safety and peace I did not overdo my visits.

There was also another Community, Franciscan Sisters, who were out on the coast in a Leprosarium. This centre, founded in 1929 by a French priest, is one of the best-known Leprosaria in Vietnam and just a good bicycle ride out of town. While he was still planning this project, the Founder went back to France to elicit the help of Religious Sisters in his work but unfortunately he died while still in France. In spite of this the Sisters who had responded to his call went out to Vietnam as they had promised and up until 1975 had run the centre by themselves. When the Communist Government came to power in 1975 they took over the Leprosarium (and all private institutions) but the Sisters stayed on nonetheless and continued their work, even though they were no longer in charge. What had been their convent is now used for administration, and the Community have a small house a little distance from the entrance of the Leprosarium.

The Centre is in an idyllic situation on the beach where patients can enjoy the natural beauty. There are large wards for men and for women, and dedicated doctors and nurses are on call full-time. Scattered around the central buildings are small family homes where families can live normal lives together and bring up their children, who more often than not, have no signs of leprosy. There is also a Primary School within the compound. For some time authorities have been trying to integrate the lepers' children into the local Secondary Schools in Qui Nhon. Unfortunately once it is known where they come from, the children are often not welcome, even though they are not infectious and their health is carefully monitored.

The patients in the Leprosarium suffer at various stages of the disease, some unable to use their hands due to the absence of all their fingers, while others hobble around on what is left of their feet. One dear old lady had benefited from help given and sat most days sewing with hands devoid of fingers. Others I met and talked with had only half their faces left or were dreadfully deformed. These were the worst cases, lucky to be there where help was available and there was someone to look after them. Later I was to find others not so lucky.

Not long after we arrived in Qui Nhon we acquired two small puppies, street dogs, which responded to tender loving care and grew very quickly on a more substantial diet than their less lucky relatives had.

Gradually our means of transport had improved. Through the help of a local priest, Fr. Peter Xuan, I was able to purchase a motor bike. With this I could carry the two dogs in a box I had made and attached to the carrier, and sometimes we went out to the beach at the Leprosarium where we would have hi-jinks in the sea! My new little Buttons caught many a chicken which he promptly buried in the sand, just for fun, no doubt, but what trouble I was in! Each time I had to run promptly to the rescue and dig it up, and worst of all, had to pay for it!

I don't know who enjoyed these excursions the most, but certainly a few hours respite from the daily problems and frustrations did a lot to keep us all sane. The roads no longer sported soldiers with guns or look-out posts but there were still problems for travellers. The repairing of punctures had long been one way for the poor to earn a pittance; now that motor-bikes had become more popular, they were a better source of income for ingenious entrepreneurs. To keep business booming, stall-holders waiting to pounce on their prey would scatter nails or sharp pieces of metal on the road. Many a time I was caught. Once I picked up a two-inch nail in my front tyre but managed to keep going that time.

I kept contact with our Sisters in Ho Chi Minh City and was overjoyed when some of them came up one weekend and we were able to have a short time together. On one occasion during the school holidays I travelled to Ho Chi Minh City by bus, a trip I would not recommend to anyone, not even the locals. When I first went down to the bus terminal I could not get anyone to sell me a ticket or tell me where I could get one. I found out later that the drivers were afraid to take foreigners. This problem had never faced them before, and they didn't know what the reaction from Government would be. I persevered however, and at last they agreed to sell me a ticket. I travelled by a local bus which probably had been on the road over twenty years; I suspect its engine was missing a few parts that were not absolutely necessary to its function of driving the wheels forward.

The bus left about three in the afternoon, due to reach Ho Chi Minh City at approximately 6.00 a.m. the following morning. The road over the pass was very winding with sheer drops to the sea on one side. I had heard yarns about trucks and buses going over the pass with either failed brakes or no brakes at all, and how the drivers drove into the judder bars all the way down to break their speeds, not something I would relish. However, we managed with divine intervention to get over safely and carried on, the only comfort stops being at the side of the road! At about 11.00 p.m. we stopped and stayed put for two to three hours. The few passengers who were still awake could not enlighten me as to the cause of the delay.

It turned out that a bridge was under repair and there was no way to continue until the job was finished. Needless to say our scheduled time of arrival was delayed and we did not get there until 9.00 or 10.00 a.m. Some of the Sisters had been waiting from 6 a.m. and had changed the guard a few times to be sure someone was there when I arrived. As soon as the bus stopped young men swarmed inside on the pretext of assisting the passengers with their luggage. We had to be watchful, as often as not all could disappear into someone else's permanent care. Wasn't I pleased to see the Sisters waiting!

Now that I was back in Vietnam, one of the things I really longed to do and had often dreamed about, was to return to Phuoc Long to find out what had happened to the people who had been in the jungle with us in war-time, and above all, to find those wonderful men who had worked and struggled with me, if any were still alive.

One day during the August vacation the Sisters arranged for transport, and a group of us went up together. I did not know what to expect. On the way I was often asked if I remembered this part of the road or that, having driven by it often in the past - but so much had changed. The one thing that did strike me was the disappearance of the jungle. The trees were gone and every scrap of land seemed under cultivation. I learned later that the jungle had been cleared from Nha Trang on the coast to the Cambodian border of Phuoc Long province. What a gigantic loss of nature in all its forms! I had encountered timber trucks on their way to the Port in Qui Nhon from where the logs were shipped out in their thousands, but I had no idea that so much jungle had been cleared. Overseas markets were now paying big money for hardwoods such as teak, still available in this area and across the border in Cambodia. What a price to pay for wealth!

We travelled for about three hours, a journey that formerly took us almost a whole day, and finally arrived in the little village of Long Dien where a group of our Sisters now lived. Our former Mission Centre had been taken over by the military in 1975 and they still occupy the compound.

Letter To The Sisters Overseas:

Aug 4th 1992

I want so much to share this experience with so many of you with whom I have already shared the journey up till now but I hope you can get the real feeling through the limitations of words and a Vietnamese typewriter.

Sunday morning, 5 a.m., it all began. Kim Phung had arranged for a car to take eight of us to Long Dien, Phuoc Long, where three of our Sisters are continuing our work with the Montagnards, started by Sr Mary Thomas, RIP, and Sr Mary Rose, who at the age of 81 accompanied us on this unbelievable journey. Sr Mary Christiane, who had lived for some years there with me, Sr Mary Celestine, who had spent some months in Long Dien, Sr Mary Germaine, home on holiday from France, Sr Mary Bernard (now known as Kim Phung), Provincial, and two young Sisters - one belonging to the village who had the opportunity of visiting her family - and me, for whom this trip was a dream I had never really allowed myself to anticipate seriously - for could it ever happen? It was happening.

We left Thu Duc 5.30/6 a.m. for a four-hour drive which once would have taken eight to ten hours. As we moved out of the Saigon area on to the country road the Sisters at regular intervals asked me, "Do you remember this road?" There was something familiar about it - the red soil perhaps - I don't know - but if this was the road I had travelled before, the scenery had changed out of recognition. The closer we got to our destination the more amazed I was at the transformation, for where previously I had seen only virgin forest and jungle was now cultivated land as far as the eye could see. Rubber trees, pepper vines, hill rice stretched for miles. Was it possible that such a change could take place in seventeen years without any kind of machinery? Only the indomitable spirit of the Vietnamese people could make such changes as this. While I marvelled at it all I suddenly caught sight - our first sight - of our mountain, Nui Ba Ra, in the distance, standing up majestic, immovable, as it had always done, and my memory immediately took me back to the day Sr M. Thomas and I stood on its top and surveyed the whole world. An American had flown us up by helicopter.

I remembered too the times I had watched planes drop bombs on it mercilessly, and I had stood spell-bound as they fell one after the other in perfect sequence, to explode in one terrible burst of flame, the roar of it reaching me only seconds later. This beautiful gift of nature from which I had seen the bodies of so many brought down from its height to be identified by relatives and taken to their final peace!

As our journey continued familiar names of places began to come back to me, names I had forgotten - Bu Nho - where I had often cycled to visit a Montagnard village.

And now we were beginning to come into very familiar ground as we turned up the road to the water-falls on the Song Be River - the shrine to Our Lady, and the last resting place of Sr M. Thomas. I saw again in memory that long procession of people who had accompanied us on foot as we took her body to that place of rest she had chosen for herself. What a beautiful spot it had been, with Nui Ba Ra in the background and the lovely Song Be River at its feet. So often on Sunday evenings we had come out here together to sit on the rocks under the trees and eat our loaf of bread. I felt sad to see the lovely trees all gone and replaced by sheds for trucks and machines. After a short search we found Sister's grave where we prayed together and I gave special thanks for having been privileged to share a short time of her life, and for all she had taught me about mission. Truly one of our great RNDMs! Sr Mary Rose was lost in memories too and her tears flowed freely, for she and M. Thomas had come together to found this mission they both loved so much.

We turned back and came to that familiar fork in the road that took us into that part of Phuoc Long that had formerly been our home. I held my breath - were we really going back? No one had said a word until I heard from the seat behind me, "Look, there's the house", and then I saw our little convent still there, looking so clean and nice amidst the mess all around it. We could not stop as it is used by the military now, but between M. Germaine and myself, we must have managed to get some photos. The lovely little dispensary is no longer there nor the workshop but the school is still standing at the end of the garden with bullet holes and shrapnel scars as we had left it. The car had kept on moving and to my disbelief was turning back - there was nowhere else to go! One dirt road that had taken us down to the river was all I could see of what I had once known as our town and village. Where there had been houses, shops, market, streets, hospital, church, military, landing strip, Government offices, etc, etc, now was a waste land covered in weeds and grass. Only those who had been part of it before would know now that it had ever existed. It truly was something I still can't fully grasp, and it brought back to me the truth - "The past is history, the future is mystery, the only reality is NOW." We had come to a dead end and as we passed our little house again

I prayed that the little we had done, the seeds we may have planted, will continue to grow.

It did not take us long to reach Long Dien village, founded in 1956 by a Catholic community who came as a body from the North with their priest, and settled there. My memory again took me back to the last time I had stopped outside its entrance. We, M. Lea, M. Dorothy and myself, were in a military jeep, being driven to we-didn't-know-where, to be released. That day the driver had stopped at the village entrance to ask the people on the road which way to go. When the people saw us they had crowded around the jeep, so pleased to see us still alive - and especially M. Lea of whom they asked many questions which at that time she preferred not to answer. We drove in past the old church I had remembered riddled with bullet holes, (and now renewed with old roofing iron), and reached our little convent.

This was the climax of our journey for here in front of the house was a group of Montagnards awaiting us. About sixteen of "my men" and their families had come from their various villages to meet me, and as I walked towards them the tears welled up and I could only look at each one and say his name which came back to me so readily, and put my arms around each one in the true sharing of God's love. Someone asked them afterwards, "What did you say when you met Sister?" and they replied, "She cried, and we all cried." We were all seventeen years older but it was as if time had stood still, hearing again that beautiful Stieng language I had come to love. There was so much I wanted to say but the lump in my throat prevented the words from coming.

Then I spotted Cay, my blind man whose little girl used to lead him into work every morning. He looked so thin, his hair gone white, dirty and unkempt. His wife and child have both died so he is left to do what he can on his own. All he wanted was a blanket because he is cold at night. This I promised to send up to him. All of them looked worn and still have a struggle to survive, and as I looked at them I wondered if any of them had ever known a time when they had enough to eat. Jian's family has grown to eight. He was still the same kind, thoughtful Jian who had shared the little rice he had with us in the jungle. I had often longed for the opportunity of thanking him and this I did with tears running down my face. Nhet, who was nurse maid and mother to Peter, Paul and Mary, was there with her own five small children, looking beautiful, tall and stately. There were so many things I wanted to ask but the time was so short and so many to love! I had taken all my photos of Peter, Paul and Mary with me and they devoured them, fascinated at how beautiful they are. They hope one day to see them in reality. They had all had a hand in rearing them, and loved them. I was so disappointed to learn after they had all gone, that one of Peter's brothers was there. I would have loved to have talked to him and given him a photo of Peter but the photos had all disappeared so quickly and I didn't have the heart to ask for them back.

The Sisters had prepared clothing and packets of food which we had taken with us, and which in their usual quiet way they had all arranged in the background. These we gave out, and by that time it was two in the afternoon; we had planned to leave again for Thu Duc at 3 p.m. I had not even had time to meet two of the three Sisters so it was time I was led into the house to share a lovely meal they had prepared for us. I was delighted to meet Sr M. John Chrysostom again as Sister had worked with us in Phuoc Long when M. Thomas became too sick to carry on that work in the dispensary. Sr M. Blandine would have been a postulant when I left Vietnam. Sr Minh Nha, a young Sister who told me she was a seventeen-year-old girl in the valley with all of us when we were caught in the cross fire in the last days of Phuoc Long. She remembers all the wounded and dying and our trying to do the little we could for them. Sister is a Long Dien girl who kept our Sisters in food when they were imprisoned in 1985. She is now an RNDM continuing the work of the Spirit with the Montagnards, travelling out each day to a Montagnard village to teach the children.

After lunch we went to pay a short visit to the Parish Priest who only this year has come back to the parish. He had been two years in our parish during my time in Phuoc Long so it was good to meet him again. And now it was time for us to leave, and we were only an hour later than we had intended! Good-byes are never easy but once we had thanked the Sisters for everything they had done to make the day so memorable, we piled in and were on our way. Everyone was very quiet, lost in their own thoughts, while I relived every moment of it again in wonder and gratitude for this gift that He had promised through Jeremiah 29/14: "I will bring you back to this land from which I have exiled you."

We did not reach Thu Duc until 8 p.m. and the Sisters were beginning to get anxious about us by that time. They were all there waiting for us, relieved to see us safely home, anxious to hear all about the day and to share with us the wonder of it all. How precious is Community!

I tried to thank Kim Phung for all she had done to make this day possible but felt my feeble "Thank you" very inadequate in contrast to how I felt - "For He who is mighty has done great things for me and Holy is His name."

The two weeks' break sped by and it was time to return to Qui Nhon again, much refreshed in body and spirit. After meeting up with my friends again and seeing the condition of most of those with prostheses, I made up my mind to get something done for them, and on my return to Qui Nhon arranged with the Rehabilitation Centre which made and fitted limbs for amputees, to help the men if we could get them over to Qui Nhon. The Sisters helped out by sending out a message by 'bush telegraph', and a group turned up ready to go. One of the Sisters accompanied them as they had to travel by bus from Phuoc Long to Ho Chi Minh City, stay the night there, and take another bus for Qui Nhon the next day.

On arrival we took them to the centre where they would stay while their homemade prostheses were being replaced. They had some time to sight-see before they set out for home again, fitted with replacements, much to their delight.

Conditions in Qui Nhon remained the same, with restrictions on our movements and on those of the locals we had become friendly with. When we got to the stage of visiting any one of these people in their homes, we soon learned that our visits were followed by those of the police, to check up on both us and them! Trust was no longer part of ordinary every-day living. Everyone had to seek permission to move from place to place, just as we did.

It did not take long before I realized that there were informers wherever I went, often from the poorer class who would be delighted to earn a few 'dong' and keep in with authorities at the same time. I soon learned to be on the alert before I spoke or replied to seemingly harmless questions. As thc time went on we became accustomed to this way of life. We put our energies into the tasks we were there for. We were foreigners to these people; they simply could not understand our ways of acting or thinking, just as we could not always accept the restrictions imposed on us that they accepted as quite normal.

My regular Saturday morning meetings with the Red Cross continued and gradually we began to get to know one another. On one occasion they said to me, "You understand us and our culture," which I felt was

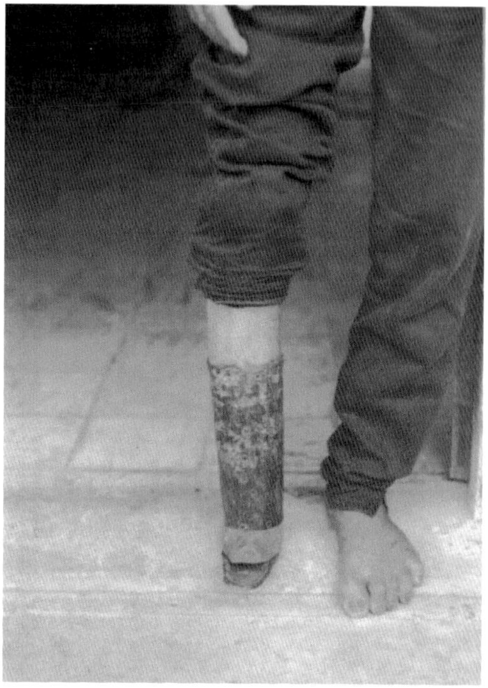

Homemade prosthesis - heavy solid wood and difficult to carry around.

a real break through. They knew I had been in the country before and that made a difference. It was not an easy task being in the middle between the team and the authorities. I was expected to know in detail what each member of the team had accomplished over the past week and exactly what they intended to do in the coming week.

On one occasion the Red Cross invited me to go out to an ethnic minority village in the hope that I might be able to help them with their water supply. We set out one day accompanied by our cadre/interpreter and met a representative of the Red Cross out there who showed me around the village which I could see was in dire straits for water. The few wells already there were insufficient for the whole village, and who can live without water? VSA kindly donated the funds needed and we were able to have six additional wells dug and furnished with pulleys and buckets in the village itself and another at the school.

The Red Cross itself was scattered around the Province, there in name but with no funds to do anything that required money. They distributed some of the aid coming in from overseas, e.g. clothing, but could do little or nothing to alleviate the real needs of the people.

Because two of our members had to travel out to the coastal village every week, VSA provided us with a four-wheel-drive Toyota vehicle. This made movement in general much easier once permission was granted to travel any distance outside our territory. The driver was supposed to manage this at his own discretion though I doubt if he ever did. He would have had to report back on every trip taken. (After thirteen years he is still driving the same vehicle for other VSA volunteers, a great record!)

Our two years' assignment at last came to an end. The other members of our Team returned home to find jobs and look again at their future, but I stayed on for another year. New volunteers came in after an assessment was made by VSA and the locals with whom we worked.

New legs made to order

My work as High School English teacher continued, as well as my job as the team co-ordinator; new members took on the old projects, except for a nurse, Helen, who came in to work with the Health Department in Hepatitis immunisation and prevention. Health-wise we ourselves were fairly lucky; we suffered from nothing more serious than boils, which some of us picked up and passed around and which kept us close to home for a while.

One weekend Helen and I decided to drive across to Pleku to visit a friend of mine who worked with the ethnic minorities there. I should have known better, but because we rarely drove ourselves anywhere I completely forgot to get permission for ourselves or for the vehicle!! We set out on our own, naively thinking that our driver deserved his weekend off too. The drive was most enjoyable until we neared the outskirts of Pleku where we were signalled by police to pull over to the side of the road. I was driving at the time and could think of no reason for the request but did not think it a good idea to refuse. We were asked for our papers.

Which papers? I handed over all that was in the car, mostly about the car! After careful scrutiny one of them piled into the back of the Toyota and gave us directions to the Police Station. We hung around there doing nothing for a few hours. There seemed to be nobody around to do official business. Eventually we were taken in to a small office where we had to answer all the customary questions:

Who were we? Where had we come from? Why had we come? etc., etc., etc. We could have avoided all this if we had chosen to pay them off, but that was not the way we operated. In the end, when they saw there was nothing in it for themselves, they allowed us to leave, with a warning to be sure to have permit papers cleared if we were visiting again!

We had both enjoyed the day to the full though - the freedom of being on our own, a luxury rarely enjoyed.

During the school holidays of that year I made a very memorable trip to North Vietnam with a group of Sisters from Thu Duc.

Chapter 8

A Pilgrimage To Our Roots In "Indo-China"
9 July 1993 - 18 July 1993

This memorable trip just happened. In April of 1993 the Vietnamese Government lifted restrictions on foreigners and it became possible for us to travel throughout the country freely. Having heard from so many of our Sisters over the years about our mission in the North I had often wished it was possible to go up to see them so that I could understand better the Faith which empowered our Sisters to endure the sufferings, struggles and the loss - and to establish such strong roots in this beautiful land.

One thing in particular that kept pushing me on was the desire to visit the grave of our Australian Sister - Sister Mary Catherine, who is buried in the grounds of a former convent in a village about 60 kilometres from Hanoi. Sister, who had been ill for over a year, died when our Sisters had to leave their missions in the wake of war in 1954 and was travelling by sampan with two other sisters endeavouring to reach Hai Phong - the large sea port, and on to Hanoi. None of our Sisters had even been able to return to visit the grave and for some reason I had this strong urge to go there. Sister Kim Phung agreed to the unplanned plan and I must say how very grateful I am to Sister and the Province for their interest and support.

There was so much to take in and so many impressions - so many stories told that the whole would fill a volume, so I will try to keep my own story as brief as possible and concentrate on our visit to former RNDM Missions.

As we neared the end of the week I felt that though we had not planned it as such, our pilgrimage North was very much part of this Centennial year, a celebration of moving in our own time, meeting the needs of the "now" within the short times we each have, so that those following on can do the same in their time with the same spirit of faith, joy and sharing of our gifts with those less fortunate.

Five of us made up a small community for the ten days sharing ourselves with each other in friendship, love and understanding, as we journeyed together - a group of RNDMs returning to their roots. I thank them for the fun, the laughter, the teasing we all gave and received in equal measure!!

Phat Diem

On Saturday, July 10th we boarded a little old Czech mini bus hired for the occasion and which served us well over the two thousand kilometres or more we travelled during the week. In spite of its rattles we only had to stop once and that was for a flat tyre. Phat Diem was our destination but I realized how unprepared I was when I saw the wonder of this place, not just a "had been" but very much an "is" in the life of the church today. The whole Church compound has been declared by the Government as an historical reserve. Suffice to say, Phat Diem in the present takes one back into another time, another culture and into a faith that has endured persecution over centuries and produced martyrs, three of whom are buried here.

Phat Diem

Daughters of St Paul

Our Sisters took over this mission from the Sisters of St Paul who ran a primary school here and in the true spirit of RNDMs met the needs of the times in various ways. But let us start at the entrance to the convent grounds which we approached along a small dirt track beside a canal. Here, Sr M. Jeanne told me the Sisters had tended many dying of starvation and sickness when food supplies had been cut off by the Japanese during World War II.

We crossed the canal by a small bridge and there in front of us was the entrance gate with the date still quite clear above - 1925. We walked through and on our left was a building which was formerly the chapel. Inside it was not difficult to recognise where the altar had been, a stone slab on the floor marks where it stood. I could easily imagine Mass being said here and the prayers that had wafted heavenward from the hearts of our Sisters.

Turning the opposite way we were confronted with a large picture of Ho Chi Minh, the Vietnamese leader! There was a table on a stand in front for meetings and forms down the centre of the chapel to seat the hospital staff who meet here each day. I stopped and prayed for all our Sisters, living and dead, who had prayed and worked here in the spirit of our Foundress Euphrasie Barbier. We wandered down the path under the trees and into the old convent on our right which now resembled a ghetto. Who could venture to make a guess at the number of families housed here? So many in each room - in not what one would call hygienic conditions! But at least they had a roof over their heads. We walked along the corridor between the kitchen, long gone, and the old refectory and along

the front verandah. I couldn't see a staircase that would take us to the top floor and we would need to climb over the people to reach it if we did find one.

We continued on down the path past buildings formerly used by our Sisters. The School, the block used for the education of the deaf and dumb, the maternity block and four or five buildings which made up the hospital, still in use. There was another separate building that had been used for retired and sick priests. And apart from all these works there were all the sidelines such as embroidery classes. These works were shared by an international community consisting of Vietnamese, French, New Zealand and Australian RNDMs.

I am sorry now I didn't have the presence of mind to visit the hospital, but there was so much to take in and so little time. As I stood in the midst of all that "had been" I was struck by the realization that all had been for the poor, the marginalized, the little people. Let it be "as it was in the beginning".

Thanh Hoa

Thanh Hoa, formerly the Provincialate and Novitiate is 175 kilometres from Hanoi so again we had to make a very early start. The countryside was magnificent and the driver most interesting with his stories of life as a soldier in the North Vietnamese Army so the time passed quickly and we were in Thanh Hoa in time for lunch, which we had amidst cement bags and scaffolding at the Bishop's house which was under construction.

News travels fast here and in no time three men arrived to talk with Sr. M. Jeanne. One was blind and had been cared for by our Sisters when he was a small boy.

A short walk from here past poor little one roomed houses we arrived at our old entrance and I am almost sure I read "Notre Dame des Missions" on the arch above it, so familiar did it seem. And there in front of us was this very impressive grey stone building clean and very well kept for it now serves as a local museum. The Novitiate stands to the left behind the trees, painted yellow, in the old French style and connected to the Provincial House by a walkway at the second floor level. My camera came out quickly and I had taken all the pictures I wanted before we were approached and told not to photograph anything yet. On our left was a smaller building at ground level which had been one of our own classroom blocks. Into this we were ushered and after being seated we went through the process of identification. As we had not prepared anything we had to concoct something on the spur of the moment, which Sr. Kim Phung did very convincingly and with ease. I was the teacher of English for the group who were taking me sightseeing during the holidays - not too far from the truth. I produced my indentification card and all was well.

We were given a guide whom we followed up the path to the impressive entrance, constructed after the Sisters left. As I passed through the front door I imagined all of us in the old habit, sweating it out and thanked God for Vatican II. Our guide wasted no time on the first floor which formerly had been used as dormitories for the older pupils to the left, with the Chapel to the right. As we were ushered along the corridor beside the chapel I noted that many of the doors had been broken and boarded up or had cupboards against them on the inside. I was disappointed that I did not get to see these rooms but we were forced to keep the "act" up and were only really interested in "museum pieces". Sr. M. Gabriel, Sr. Kim Phung, and I fled ahead hoping the rest of the group could get lost as we were terrified that Sr. M. Jeanne or someone would forget and start asking questions. We climbed the stairs at the end of the corridor and I noticed that they were in iron and not in stone as we have everywhere now. We were now on the second floor which formerly had been classrooms. They had been transformed into typical museum showrooms with very interesting displays of ancient Vietnamese history which our guide was delighted to share with us. I could easily have got lost in it all if I had not kept thinking - 'my Sisters lived and worked here 40 years ago' - hard to believe. My eyes and my mind kept wandering as I tried to visualize what it must have been like. Then I would bring myself back to try and look intelligent while Sr. Kim Phung interpreted for me and Sr M. Gabriel. We smiled sweetly and nodded at the appropriate times. We were reminded a few times that the car was waiting for us but we were really in no hurry to leave. Just before we were about to leave we were taken over to a model of a hill with a river at its base. "Here," she recounted, "47 American planes were shot down in one day". I'm sure she really believes it!!!

We patted the heads of the royal elephants in the grounds as we left and I thanked God for all the good things He had allowed to happen here and especially for all the wonderful Vietnamese Sisters we have who had worked here and grown in faith as RNDMs.

Lang Son

This mission is about a six hour trip of 200 kilometres through exquisite mountainous scenery and I wondered how long the trip must have taken in the past. Lang Son is the town nearest to the Chinese border which we were most fortunate to see.

We eventually arrived at our old mission compound with nothing familiar to tell us we were there. Only after roaming around for a while did I notice our old traditional wall still standing around the section. The only part of the old convent left here is a corner - a part of two walls, and two or three steps to a doorway. It had been a two storey building, not

Lang Son near the Chinese Border

very large, which had been destroyed during the American bombing raids. We could see on the ground where a smaller building had stood in front, maybe the entrance and parlours. Down the right hand side coming from the gate there had been a school block also completely destroyed. On the left opposite is the only existing part of the original, an old classroom building, small and narrow which serves as the parish church, for that too was destroyed completely together with the Bishop's house.

We met the Bishop here in a small, long, extremely simple house. He himself had been imprisoned for 31 years because he had been consecrated without the permission of the Government. He was only released in 1991. Here too, we met a woman 104 years of age, full of life; still tending her rice fields. In the past she had worked for our Sisters, cooked for 25 priests and took food daily to the Bishop all the time he was in prison. An extraordinary character.

It was sad to see the rubble - remains of all that had been, but the simplicity of the present seemed to compensate for that and I can only hope it can remain as is with the old church bell hanging from the branch of a large tree that would have been there in our time.

The North Vietnamese still adapt their bicycles to carry heavy loads as they did during the war.

Chapter 9

The Last Resting Place Of Sister Mary Catherine

We knew the name of the town, and that the building which had formerly been the convent of the local sisters was now in use as the local hospital, but that was all. Where was Sister Catherine buried? As no RNDMs had been there since their departure in 1954 we knew it would be hard to locate her grave.

After an eventful drive along the muddy top of a dam and through the rice fields because we took the wrong road, we stopped and had lunch with a priest who wouldn't take "no" for an answer. He was the priest of a poor country parish where the people had been without a priest for forty years. Father himself had spent two and a half years in prison because he had been ordained without Government permission and over lunch he told his story which at times moved him to tears.

We travelled on from there to a town called Hung Yen where we met an old man who had been the gardener in the hospital grounds and who remembered the wooden cross and where it had stood - long gone. The hospital itself was only around the corner but so as not to draw attention to ourselves some of the Sisters went in first while we remained in the car. On their return Sr. Kim Phung told me where to look and I walked through the gate wondering what to expect. Just inside to the right was a large garden block with a good variety of weeds growing in it so I couldn't even pretend I was admiring the flowers. On the far side I saw three young trees Sister had told me to look for and I walked around as inconspicuously as I could. Sure enough the middle tree was growing on a raised mound higher than the rest of the garden. "If it was just the garden it surely would have been levelled off long ago," I thought as I prayed a hasty prayer for Sister hoping that one day in the near future her remains may be brought here to Thu Duc to be buried with our other RNDMs.

It would have been foolish to have tried to photograph anything here though I would dearly have loved to do so and I quickly and quietly returned to the waiting car full of gratitude for having been able to accomplish this important part of our pilgrimage to the North.

> *When I was in Thu Duc in 1969 I happened upon a home for the elderly run by some Sisters in a place called Honai. I often used to go out there, especially when supplies were arriving from New Zealand and give them soap and things I felt they would appreciate. I took Sr. M. Gerard and Sr. M. Vianney out there when they called in on their way home from the Chapter. While there one day I met a Sister who told me that she had been at Hung Yen Convent when one of our Sisters was buried there in 1954. I did not get into details at that time but always remembered her telling me. Sadly we still have no proof that Sister's grave is where we think.*

Before we left Hanoi three of us went over to visit the Sisters in whose guest house our own sisters had been staying, to meet the Superior and thank her. During that conversation Sr. M. Jeanne asked if I wanted to say anything and to my surprise I heard myself asking if they were the same order of sisters as those in Honai. They weren't but as the conversation went on we ended up with the Sister's name and that she belonged to the Dominican Sisters. Surely Sr. M. Catherine is taking over.

Chapter 10

From The Past To The Present - Dai Lam

How does one start to describe this poor little country parish, situated 90 kilometres from Hanoi and the centre of our Sisters return to the North on Mission? Here two young Sisters are working with the present parish priest who jokingly refers to himself as 'only half a priest'. He was ordained without Government permission so was ordered to return to his family and, in other words, 'get lost'. He came back to this little village where he had been born and lived with the then parish priest until he later died. After that Father continued to run the parish and has been doing so unofficially for the past thirteen years. I was most impressed by his vision, his knowledge and acceptance of present day thinking of the Church and his courage to try to implement change.

The Church building had never been completed and is boarded up at the top to stop the rain coming in.

I was struck by the absence of statues and adornments in the sanctuary and found them stacked away in a small room at the back. Father had been to the South only once and then in quest of some religious sisters who would help him in this little out-of-the-way parish. Every congregation he approached turned him down and he had given up when it was suggested that he try our Sisters. Our two Sisters work here in the parish with the women and young girls and assist them in so many aspects of life.

There are numerous poor little buildings built in the 1920's scattered around the compound. These are being used to capacity now, with the Sisters teaching catechism and training women and girls in kindergarten work.

This is education of the poor in reality. Some of these women, up to 40 years of age and unmarried, come from villages as far away as 200 kilometres to spend three to four months with the Sisters. After that they return to their own villages to instruct their own and to set up kindergartens. Father himself has a group of boys of all ages who desire to be priests. They too stay here and receive instruction as well as lessons in French from an elderly man - Saigonese - who has offered his services for three years.

We were welcomed in real Vietnamese style with old traditional songs from the North, saw the little ones who came to kindergarten bedded down for siesta - no family planning here! - and then were invited to partake of a feast shared by everyone - the whole big family squeezed into a small makeshift dining room. It was great.

There is no special house built for the Sisters who share a dark little partitioned off end of a larger room. Here there is room for two beds and a shelf. No different from any other part of the housing. The plan is not to remain here but to move on when there is no longer the need. At 1.30 p.m. the bell rang and everyone went to the Church for evening prayer. By two o'clock the little ones were wide awake again and everyone gathered to entertain us before we had to return to Hanoi. It was beautiful to see the simplicity of each group and as I watched them I marvelled at the courage of these simple people who have hung on to what they firmly believe in spite of the difficulties and risks this entails. I marvel too at the understanding of our Sisters in following our revised Congregational Documents. When I asked about this I was told they studied them carefully. I am more inclined to think that they did far more than study them. They must have literally devoured them, so well have they understood them.

Chapter 11

Continuing My Life's Work In Thu Duc

By October 1994 my VSA contract in Qui Nhon was completed and I prepared to move on to Ho Chi Minh City and return home. However, once I had reached Thu Duc and spoken with Sister Provincial, plans began to change. Would I stay and teach the Sisters English?

I wasn't quite sure just what that would entail, but if that was the direction in which the Lord was leading I was prepared to follow, the Provincial in New Zealand agreed if I could find another teaching job through which I could get Government permission to stay.

This all took some weeks to do and entailed privately visiting teachers whom the Sisters knew, and eventually making contact with the Principal of the Thu Duc University where evening classes were held for students and workers. Fortunately the University was more than pleased to use the gifts of an English speaker. So I was set up for the time being with all the permits except one - to help the Sisters in Thu Duc and Thi Nghe and also the Novices. Many of them had been attending classes but I found they lacked understanding; most of their learning had been by rote, and they were being taught incorrect pronunciation.

Gradually I worked myself into this new pattern of life, living again in community as far as I could. Because the evening classes ran from

5.30 p.m. until 9.00 p.m. I had to arrange my evening prayer and meals apart from the other Sisters. After a month or two I began to feel very uneasy: I knew that government regulations expressly forbade foreigners to live with any Religious in their houses. I had discussed this often with some of the Sisters who had enough English to understand, and also with Sister Provincial, but none of them seemed too worried. They were on very good terms with the local police whose own children were at the Sisters' Kindergarten. However, I knew that in time someone would catch up with us - and what then?

Every day I walked around the streets, both for exercise and to see what might be available in the form of alternative accommodation. One day I found a small house for sale not far from the convent. The owner's family had received permits to leave the country to join relatives in the United States. The only money available was that which I had saved up from my allowance whilst in Qui Nhon working with VSA. It was only a pittance compared to what was needed. One of the Sisters accompanied me to talk to the owners, but I could see that if we did find the money needed, we would be buying more land, while in the Thu Duc compound we already had more than we needed!

In the end we all agreed that we could build a small house out in the garden beside the Novitiate, and if ever there was a problem we could demonstrate to those who needed to know that I was not living with the Sisters. We went ahead with that plan, calling our building 'the hut' - a hut needed no building permit. 'The Hut' was my home for the next nine years.

Dot, one of our boarders from Phuoc Long days very ill with cancer, RIP.

I still had my motorbike, I could not have functioned without it and during a break in the teaching curriculum I was anxious to visit Phuoc Long again. I wanted to renew contact with the villages. On a motorbike that was much easier to do. It was inconspicuous and less expensive. At that stage I was no longer sure of the road so I invited Sister Provincial to accompany me. She agreed and we set out hoping to arrive at our mission station within four or five hours.

With not much traffic in the way of vehicles, the trip was fairly straight-forward until we came to crossroads - which way now? I stopped the bike and without getting off I turned to ask Sister's advice. She wasn't sure of directions either, so I decided to take a right turn and ask someone on the way. We sped off up the road for a long way until I met another crossroads. I turned again to ask Sister which direction to take. To my horror I found she was not there! Where could she be? Not on the pillion! Not on the road! Not anywhere in sight! I hadn't felt or heard her fall! Surely she hadn't got off away back there!

I turned the bike and sped back over the ground praying that I had not lost her for good. Miles flew by and then I saw a bike in the distance coming towards me. Much to my relief there was Sister safe and sound on the back. At our last stop she had got off the bike to ask for directions and to her astonishment I had sped off without her. It would have made an hilarious shot for television!

We laughed so hard it took us a while to get control again and find our right course. After another stop (for a puncture) we finally did arrive safe and sound at our mission. Were we glad to get off the bike and enjoy the company of the Sisters.

We stayed the night, I contacted my friend Nhet, and we made arrangements to visit the villages the next time I came up. Now I knew the way and felt secure. Nhet had been a valuable part of the workshop before 1975. As a young girl she had been employed to look after our orphan babies during the day. She had also accompanied them and the Sisters to Saigon just before Phuoc Long fell. Now she was a married woman with four children of her own. When she could, she worked for the Sisters, who were now running a boarding school for ethnic minority children who were attending the State schools.

Nhet and her husband having a break in the rubber plantation

On my many visits later Nhet and her husband would accompany me on their motorbike to the different villages where I met up with many of the men who had been involved in the workshop. During these trips I would stay maybe two nights with the Sisters, all the time aware that my presence if detected could be penalised, though this village is entirely Catholic and easily accessible.

The more frequent my visits, the more I could see the destitution and poverty in which the people were still struggling to survive. With each successive trip, the greater was the load of material help to be carried. There is a limit to what one can carry on a motorbike, I had to find another way!

One day I was introduced to a wonderful Vietnamese man who ran a small fleet of vehicles for hire, including a larger station-wagon type. This he hired to me once or twice a month as the need demanded, and he drove me to the villages during the dry season. Once the rains came and his vehicle could no longer negotiate the mud, we would drive up to a point just outside the town where we changed into an old army jeep which could cope with the roads. No problem! Both of these drivers became great friends and supporters and I relied on their sensible opinions in many matters.

Co Yen my friend and trusty translator and Anh Trang our jeep driver and general factotum.

Once people learned of the needs, funds were donated from various places, including the New Zealand Consulate, the British Consulate, the Organisation of Expatriate Women, Hotel Saigon, Church groups based overseas, Schools and Parishes in England and Ireland and various private benefactors. All this generosity was what really made the difference. Very rarely have I had to ask directly for funds.

Gradually my works with the ethnic minority people in the villages increased; and I was also involved in setting up a shelter in Saigon for prostitutes. As the centres grew and provided better opportunities for assistance, I found my teaching commitments an increasing burden. At last I resigned from the English classes and found other ways of obtaining a Visa every six months. My jeep driver became my manager in Phuoc Long; he was the one who got things done in the villages between my visits. He saw to business with the town Council and village leaders. He was well known in the town and knew all

The children are happy in spite of the harsdship they endure daily

the business people. Through various channels we approached the Council equivalent for assistance in improving the water supply.

When I had seen the misery and destitution of the village on my return in 1995, I knew that health had to be a priority, starting with water and housing. The village chief (chosen and appointed by Vietnamese Government Officials) was happy for four large water filters to be constructed over various natural springs around the village. All I had to do was pay the cost once we were satisfied with the finished product. It was interesting to note that once these filters were installed, the rate of diarrhoea and deaths among the children dropped considerably and we were no longer bombarded for medication each time we showed up.

There were many other health problems to deal with - malnutrition, hepatitis, tuberculosis, malaria, to name a few and on many occasions I was grateful for the assistance of two doctor friends, one a Canadian and the other a New Zealander, who would accompany me and assist with their expertise. We found at least seven T.B. patients here in the last stages of the disease. Over the years all but one have died in spite of the medication prescribed. Luckily in this village I found no leprosy. Other places were not so fortunate.

Montagnard housing was appallingly poor. With their former building materials, thatch and bamboo, now almost completely wiped out,

T.B. Patients. RIP

Minh with vehicle

their traditional long houses were a thing of the past. Whereas formerly the extended family would live together, now only immediate members could fit into the small space of each hut. During the monsoon season it was impossible to escape from the wet and damp. The earthen flooring was saturated through and through, the water turning it into sticky mud. The people built bamboo platforms above this mess in order to make a 'dry' living area.

One little boy in donated clothes

On the other hand, in the dry season the earth was like fine red talcum powder. Red dust covered everyone and everything.

For two or three years the Government gave each village a number of "Housing Kits" for the most destitute. Each of these consisted of nine concrete uprights, timber for the roofing frame and some corrugated iron for the roof. Nothing was provided as walls or as flooring. So with the agreement of the village chief we provided flooring in the way of tiles, once the floor had been raised enough to prevent the water from running through. Some of the people who could find enough bamboo built outside walls; a few others who had access to timber were able to build up a more lasting home.

The daughter and granddaughter of Thi Linh, a leper patient, who live in the village but apart from their mother.

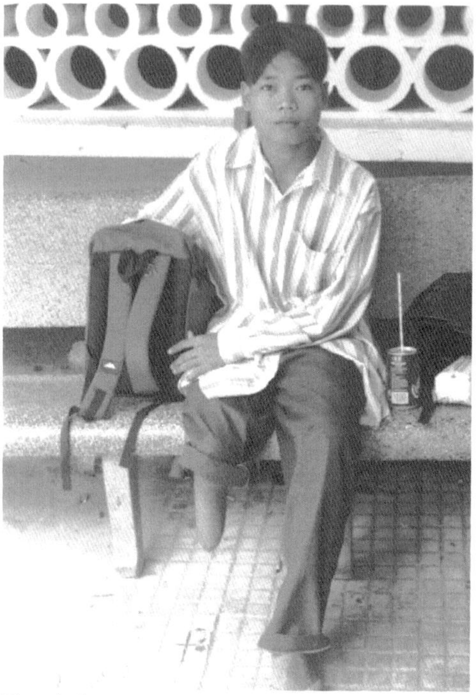

Diem before...

...and after

With some funds still available I offered to supply this village with fourteen more similar "Housing Kits" for the many more needy families who had missed the government hand-outs. The chief was agreeable to this until the next time I returned to make arrangements. In my absence apparently he had discussed my proposition with his Vietnamese counterparts; they would agree to my going ahead only if I paid for a permit. Sorry, no way! I was not going to waste our

The village water supply before...

...and after

precious funds on greedy officials. So the village missed out on more houses because of the greed of the few.

In the village I found one young boy, a fifteen-year-old, hobbling around on one leg aided by a stick from the bush. It seems that when he was only four years old he had been out in the jungle with his father when they were both attacked by a venomous snake. His father died from this encounter; little Diem had his leg amputated to save his life. No-one had ever suggested that he get a prosthesis, so on my return to Saigon I contacted a Rehabilitation Centre and made arrangements for him to come back with me on my next trip. After some weeks there being fitted and practising walking, he returned to his village a new person, very proud of himself and amazingly agile on his new limb.

There were two other cases in this village which stand out in my memory. One was a woman who had given birth to her baby but was unable to get up or move. A huge stomach swelling and her jaundiced colour were sure signs of severe hepatitis. What to do? I called on one of my trusty doctors who agreed to return to the village within the week with me just to see if there was anything we could do for her. In those few days her health had deteriorated even more and the doctor feared she had only a week to live at the most. She was at the stage where she needed proper hospital treatment and care but now, too late! No money!

We had to leave her, feeling pretty useless in the face of things. I returned to the village again the following month and asked the family about her. I expected to hear about her funeral. To my utter astonishment they told me she was out helping in the rice field. I found this hard to believe and asked one of the children to go and find her. She duly arrived, certainly looking somewhat different from how she had looked a month before. She now had a terrible cough for which she asked me to give her some medicine. (I was so completely taken up with asking her what she had done to get better that in the end I think I forgot to give her something for the cough!)

It appears that the family had called in one of their own village doctors or, as we would call them, "traditional healers". She showed me pieces of bark from various plants and trees that were given to her to boil up and drink the infusion. Apparently this was the cure! We were astounded, but whatever it was, she was certainly better, at least for the time being.

Another woman I had known for a long time had been one of the T.B. patients who had responded particularly well to the T.B. programme. She was expecting another baby, her fourth or fifth. When I saw her one day we talked about the baby arriving soon. A few days later I heard that she was in a hospital in Saigon. I couldn't believe it. This must be really serious! I set out to find her. It was not an easy task even to find the hospital that was the largest hospital in Ho Chi Minh City, catering for patients throughout the whole country. With few clues as to her whereabouts or her condition, it was going to be 'touch and go' whether I would ever catch up with her. I tramped up and down and around and in and out of wards. And there suddenly was my good friend, her husband! He had been sitting with her when he saw me come in and relief spread all over his face.

The wife was very poorly as they told me the story: it seems she gave birth at home in the village to a little baby girl, but there were

We assisted with providing raised floors for villagers

complications and the midwives could not stop the bleeding. In the middle of the night they found someone to take her and her husband in to the small Medical Centre in the town. When the staff there saw her condition they didn't want her on the premises for fear that she would die while with them. They promptly put her in an ambulance and sent her and her husband off to Ho Chi Minh City, a journey of four to five hours at that time of night.

When I arrived she had already been operated on. I could not understand, though, why she was now lying out at the end of a corridor where spare beds were stored. I soon learned from both her husband and some of the patients in the ward that because they had no money, no-one would consider doing any more for them. The poor husband had nothing to eat and no money to buy anything. I sent him post-haste to the nearest shop while I tried to talk to the poor woman. All that was worrying her was her baby, whom she hadn't even seen yet, and the other children at home on their own. I found the doctor on the ward and was told they couldn't do any more for her, or wouldn't! I thought.

Villagers today - for many little has improved

I offered to take them both back up to the hospital in Phuoc Long

One of our friends born with only one arm and a deformed leg.

as soon as I could find a car. At this he offered me an ambulance, probably afraid I would follow up this case and get him into trouble. (Even some of the other patients were going to report him, so there was no time or need for me to get involved further). We moved down to the ground floor with their meagre possessions, and Trang in a wheelchair.

An ambulance arrived with driver and nurse to accompany the patient. But I could not believe it! Neither driver nor nurse would lift a finger to help get this very sick woman into the ambulance. Trang was a Stieng tribal woman and they would not touch her. It was left to her husband and me to do what we could to lift her up into the back of the vehicle, struggle over an oxygen tank taking up all the floor space, and lift her again on to the stretcher. How she survived all that, and without a murmur, I don't know.

I could not go up with them at that stage as I had my motorbike with me and no-one at home would know where I was. I promised to come up as soon as I could to see how they were. This I did in a day or two, and found they had taken her to a new hospital, just opened and in the throes of 'getting into action'. She was in a ward there, and clean. That was an improvement in her care but I could see she had little time left in this life. All she wanted to do was to return to her village and see her little baby. I encouraged her husband to take her home but the doctor assured him she would be better left in hospital - they could help her! I left money with them for medication and expenses in general. When I returned a few days later she had passed away.

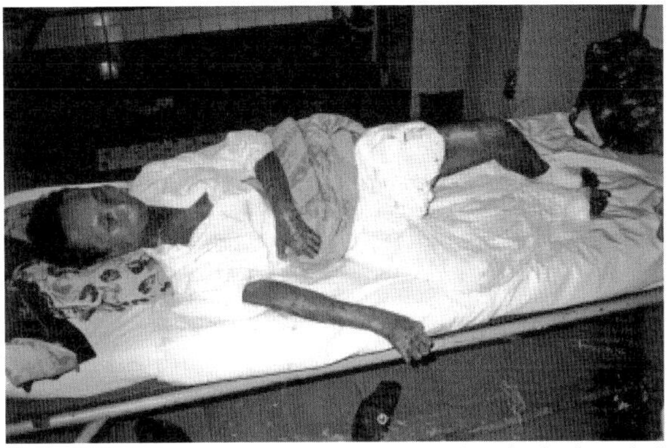

A leper patient in the hospital

Once I knew that, my concern was for the baby and I set off on my next trip praying that someone was looking after her. I was armed with supplies of baby milk powder and a bottle. I knew the family would have none. Thank God the little thing was alive but living on rice water only, fed through a filthy bottle tied up with rubber bands. She was looked after by an elderly man whom I had known for years. He had broken a hip which had never been seen to and moved around as best he could on a homemade crutch. From first glance I knew I would have to get someone, a woman, to look after the baby properly. The poor husband was doing his best for the four other children. He was happy to ask someone to bc 'mother' for the time being. We negotiated together with a woman we both knew and I agreed to pay her so much and supply the milk powder needed. It was amazing to see how the little bundle of life survived and progressed and I wonder how she is now years later.

While there was plenty to keep me busy in this village, I also had commitments in three or four other villages where some of the men lived and where I found Leper patients. These were the most desperately needy people I found anywhere - they had no-one to turn to even for the most basic necessities. They existed on the outskirts of their villages and relied entirely on the charity of someone in the village to give them rice and water for the day.

The first woman I found lay on the ground in a thatched shelter. A water jar was outside the hut. People filled that for her but, apart from that, no-one would go near her for fear of catching the disease. One of her feet was twisted and she could not walk so she was completely

Phom's home when we found her

confined to that space. Her life was only a wretched existence. She was called merely "Phom," meaning "Leper" in their language.

Over the years, with assistance from the different groups of donors, we were able to build her a decent house and take her to the Leprosy Hospital where she had her foot straightened. She was able to walk again and even to smile again. Every month I would visit her and take enough rice, meat, and vegetables to keep her going until I returned. We had special shoes made for her in Saigon that would fit all that was left of her feet after her toes had disappeared. Her poor hands were as crippled as her feet. She was always so grateful and often said how sorry she was that she had nothing to give us in return.

I suppose the most heart-breaking patients I found were a family in which three of the children were afflicted with leprosy, Hansen's Disease, as it's called in medical terms. The oldest member, a young man of thirty years, was married with three young children of his own; Yum, his sister, was twenty two years old, and a younger brother was nineteen. They all lived together with their mother, the father having died of leprosy some years before.

The Leper patient, Phom, as we found her...

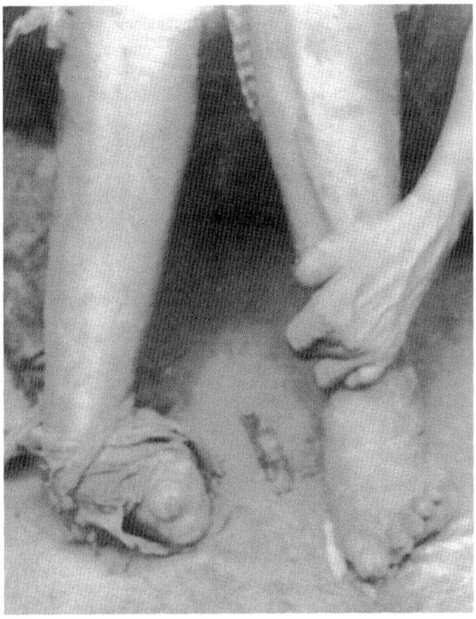

...her hands and feet

I happened to be visiting their village when I came across them. Never have I seen such hopelessness on the faces of young people as I saw that day. I talked to the youngest, who told me that he contracted leprosy when he was nine years old and had never, over those ten years, seen a doctor or been given medicine of any kind. He was finding it difficult to walk as one leg was badly affected and he had a terrible ulcer under his foot. All three had trouble with their hands and could not grasp or hold things well. Consequently when going out to cut bamboo shoots for food they often cut their legs with the bush knives. We arranged to have better housing built for both families and provided them with monthly supplies of food. In the end we were able to get all three to the Leprosy Hospital (originally established and run by the Sisters of Charity who still work there under employment) where they received help for ulcers and for their general health. After some weeks in hospital Yum and her older brother returned home but Sarang, the

Phom - after having her foot straightened in hospital

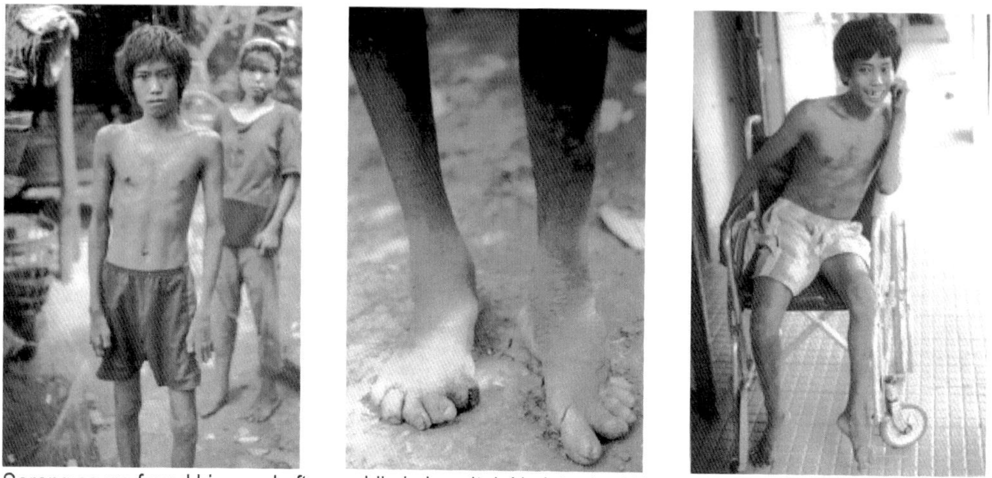

Sarang as we found him, and after a while in hospital. He later had his left leg amputated.

younger brother stayed on while doctors tried to get his damaged leg back into action.

Their efforts were unsuccessful and there was nothing they could do but to amputate the leg. He came through this very well but was now left with only one leg and his fingers closed up. What could he do? The hospital decided to give him a room there where he lives permanently, though he visits his family on special occasions like the New Year Tet. He is a very intelligent young man and can compose music and sing. I only wish I had had time to encourage him to develop his gifts.

Yum when we found her...

...later at the hocpital

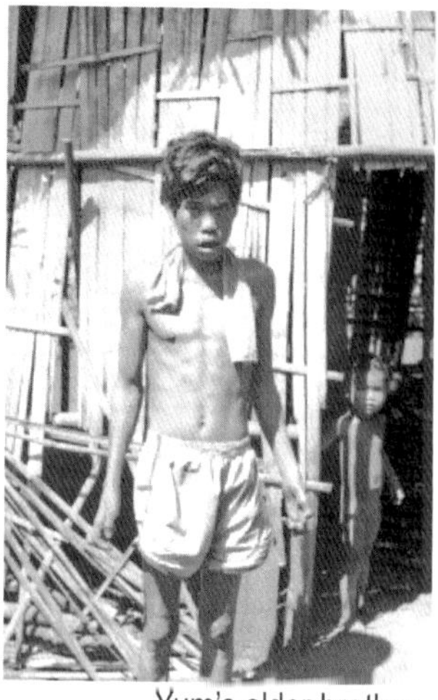

Yum's older brother.

Bath time for Yum's baby.

We gave the family some calves and a bull which they reared and cared for. Now they have a number of stock which they can sell as income. The older brother, in spite of his handicaps, works the little land he has and has planted nut trees which should also supplement the income. A shelter for the cattle in the monsoon season was also set up. From this they can use the manure they gather on their land.

In this village also, out of our own donated funds, we provided five more 'house kit-sets' for the desperately needy, only to have them confiscated by the police and never returned! The excuse given was that we didn't have permission from the authorities to give them out, which was true. We knew we would never get permission if we did ask.

One of the former workers lived here also and we provided him with a calf and a bull. On one of my visits I found that the cow had given birth to a bull calf and I suggested that he sell it as two males together would give him trouble one day but he wouldn't hear of it, such was his attachment and love for his animals!

In the fourth village I found another three patients in more or less the same conditions as the other lepers. Two women were existing in

One of our leper patients with her prized livestock

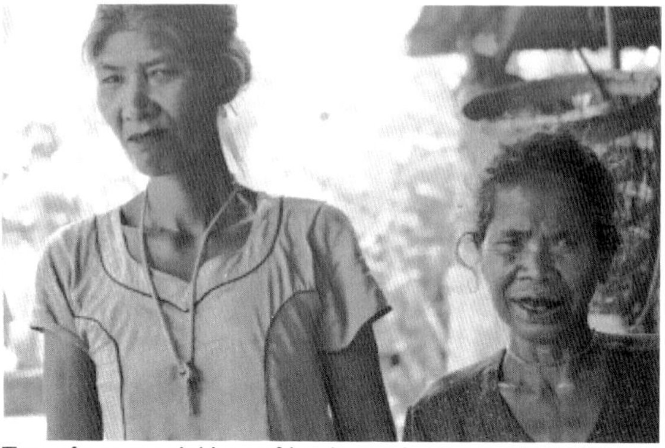

Two of our special leper friends to whom we gave cattle and chickens.

what was left of a house and barely living on whatever food they could beg from the village. A sick man also lived here by himself. He had been in the French army at one stage and he tried to converse in French whenever he met a foreigner but even those who could speak French fluently could not quite understand what he was saying. The usual monthly food distribution was set up here also. After building them each better housing, I offered them some chickens to raise and sell. The two women looked after them well and had great success. The flock multiplied in leaps and bounds, so we offered them also a calf and a bull, which they looked after like their children.

They took turns each day at taking them out to graze and the animals thrived. The bull grew so big I would not venture too close to him nor would anyone in the village, but the owners could do what they liked with him. A shelter for the cattle was built at the back of the house and a run for the chickens where they could be locked in at night to stop the fowls being stolen by the youth of the village.

They had a calf ready to sell when I went back on one of my trips and they told me of their misfortune. No-one would buy from them because they were lepers! I promptly bought it off them and gave it to another group without any more trouble.

At various times we helped the women to get to the Leprosy Hospital for some weeks where they could have a health check-up, after which they would return home to their happier manner of living.

Medication was made available through the Health Department and the local hospital but it had to be collected personally by the patient

The huge bull everyone was scared of!

each month. This was almost an impossibility. More often than not, they were completely oblivious of the day of the week, or even which month it was; these people did not have clocks or calendars and many were illiterate. None of the people in these far-flung villages had means of transport or money to pay someone to take them to the hospital on a motorbike.

In the young, medication will arrest the disease and prevent further tissue damage, but most of our patients were past that stage; their leprosy had stabilized spontaneously and apart from ulcers forming under their feet it would not worsen. Limb and tissue loss would never recover of course.

Our small successes and developments were not entirely without problems. Once or twice while in the villages I was summoned to the police station to give an account of my presence, but on the whole we were not bothered too much in that way.

Sr Sheila O'Toole on her return to Vietnam with two old friends

Towards the year 2000 and onwards there was a movement of unrest in the Highlands all over the country, especially in the North East and this eventually grew into an unprecedented protest. The Ethnic Groups complained ineffectually to the Government about their land being taken by the Vietnamese to plant coffee trees. At last the Montagnards walked into the town as a body to protest officially and be heard, only to be met with police, batons and bullets. Unofficially over two hundred people were killed, though that kind of news never reaches the media, either inside or outside the country. The surviving protesters were then herded back into their villages, with no one permitted either to leave or to enter the area.

Troubles Reported In Vietnam's Tribal Hill Regions

Journalists returning from a tour of Vietnam's central highlands, say there is little sign that land disputes between the government and minority hill tribes are subsiding.

Last month indigenous groups launched a series of dramatic protests against the loss of their traditional lands to cash crop farmers who have migrated from the low lands.

The Vietnamese Government immediately barred foreigners from visiting the area.

This prompted the US State Department to warn that ratification of the US-Vietnam trade agreement could be affected if Vietnam did not allow independent reporting on the situation.

However as Tricia Fitzgerald reports, when the Foreign Ministry took foreign journalists on a tour of the region, reporters were not allowed any contact with disgruntled hill tribes.

FITZGERALD: Journalists taken to the Vietnamese Central Highlands last week say the tour was a frustrating exercise which didn't live up to the 'open access' promises of the Foreign Ministry.

With no ethnic protestors in sight - the journalists were instead treated to a display of military might at a government celebration in the hill tribe town of Pleiku.

The Agence France Press (AFP) news agency's correspondent Steve Kirby who was on the trip says, although there was no contact allowed with ethnic protestors, local officials did confirm the large scale of the unrest.

KIRBY: This was the first time they'd admitted any foreign media to the Central Highlands since they sent in the army six weeks ago to try and get to grips with this wave of protests.

They started at the beginning of February with a series of demonstrations that swept the main towns of the region.

And they made a great fanfare about finally admitting journalists down there. But despite their promises in advance that they would allow us to get both sides of the picture and to talk to some of the members of the minorities who demonstrated, they completely renegged on those undertakings.

And they only took us to tourist villages which were entirely controlled: there was an enormous presence of plain clothes security people accompanying us at all times.

We were taken into the region and out of the region escorted by uniformed police - so every effort was made to limit our ability to report independently.

But from those trips that we were ... the brief stops and snatched interviews we were able to conduct outside their control, it was really very evident that the problems are still going on.

And despite this massive six week old deployment of plain clothes security men and in some areas the armed forces - they really have yet to get to grips with the protests among the minorities.

FITZGERALD: You were saying that you were able to snatch some interviews ... who were you able to speak to?

KIRBY: There were one or two officials who were willing to admit that the scale of the problem really was much bigger than was being let on and who were willing to express their concerns about the implications for the future.

One official told us privately that he reckoned it would take decades for the authorities to get to grips with the hostility of the indigenous minorities towards the ethnic Vietnamese.

We were told that there'd been violent clashes just a week previously, just to the west of one of the main towns that we'd visited.

It was quite clear concordant statements from local residents and from officials in private - it was made quite clear that six weeks on, this unrest is still going on in the countryside ... and the main towns are only under control because of the massive presence of plain clothes security and because of concerted efforts to stop people coming in from the countryside to protest.

FITZGERALD: Were you able to get any indication of what sort of casualties or arrests have taken place?

KIRBY: Well, the authorities insist that they were very, very small scale. We were told that in one province they'd arrested just twenty people and that of those, thirteen had been released.

Given the scale of the protests, it is quite evident that the arrests must have been on a far, far greater scale.

One village that we were taken to - the village notice board was full of wanted posters: there were a dozen outstanding arrest warrants that were displayed on the notice board - so it's quite clear to me that the arrests were on a large scale.

FITZGERALD: Steve Kirby says hill tribes dependent on tourism have been hard hit by the government's closure of the area to outside visitors. He says news that close to one hundred thousand Vietnamese - who are to be displaced by a hydro dam in the north - are to be shipped into the area, is creating the fuel for more protests in the future.

But is the vital trade pact with the US likely to be affected by the government's handling of the hill tribe revolt?

The AFP's Vietnam correspondent Steve Kirby thinks not.

KIRBY: It's certainly possible and I think probable that, given the bipartizan support for free trade in the US Congress, that this agreement probably will be ratified - but I think it will be ratified against a background of mounting criticism.

And the ratification is likely to take longer than was originally envisaged by its supporters.

First broadcast on 20 March 2001
Australian Broadcasting Corporation

At the same time we were beginning to find that our movements in the hills were not as free as they had been. We were advised to lie low for a bit until the political situation calmed down. We tried to do that, but knowing how desperate people would be for food we had to take the risk and distributed our goods discreetly, fortunately without problems that time. The powers-that-be were afraid that foreigners or outsiders would stir up the people to stand up for their rights and cause another uprising. My trusty jeep driver began to have visits from the police asking what we did in the villages and who we contacted. Conditions were getting more difficult all round.

At this point we thought it advisable to approach the Province Centre, meet with officials, and obtain a permit for what we were doing to forestall any more trouble. After a lot of negotiating the People's Committee consented to meet with us and we put our case forward, a request for official permission to visit the Ethnic Minority villages to assist with housing, water and general needs.

I cannot tell you how many visits we made to that office, sometimes to pick up a policeman who would have to accompany us to the villages to check out exactly what we were doing and who we would be making contact with. At other times we had to report in detail on our movements but at no time would they give us, either verbally or in writing, a permit to assist our people. Later they came up with a proposition: would I help another village of Ethnics who had recently been moved in from the border areas? Before we agreed to this we naturally asked to be taken there first to see the situation. After seeing the needs, always the basics, housing and water, and after discussions with my own team we decided to get involved not only with the village but also with the People's Committee members. This could do no harm we thought, and maybe a little good!

All this time we continued to visit our other villages and leper patients with permission. We financed about ten to fourteen houses and dug wells, one for every two families throughout the village. Everything had to be built exactly to the specifications set by the Government so we were not free to provide anything outside their plans. A corrugated iron roof was provided for each house. One family told me they had never met up with such a thing in all their lives and when the first monsoon rains came and pelted on the new roof they were so terrified by the noise that they ran out into the downpour in fear for their lives.

As the days went by we struggled on, side-stepping problems where we could, and in the process meeting up with many good people who would give a hand wherever they could.

Once during the earlier years of this time in Vietnam when I was on a flight in to Ho Chi Minh City I met Paula Kelly, who at that time was the co-ordinator of "CARE International" in Ho Chi Minh City. After a few passing words as we boarded the flight she gave me her business card. Paula is a criminologist with experience in working in women's prisons in Australia.

For me this turned out to be the beginning of a great friendship and also the beginning of involvement in a project I would never have envisaged myself - but that did not happen until later.

CARE International in Vietnam is a CARE mission supported by CARE Australia. Paula was involved in the development of one of CARE's projects in Vietnam, 'Skills for Incarcerated Women', which aimed at developing personal skills (and therefore self-sufficiency) in former prostitutes sentenced to rehabilitation. This project was funded by Oxfam Netherlands, NOVIB, to provide training in computers, small-business skills, health, (particularly women's health, with emphasis on HIV/AIDS and STDs), arts, drama, photography and English; it also provided all the equipment needed for these classes and obtained suitable outside tutors in each area.

It was at that time when I was involved with teaching and also trying to help the Leper patients that I found myself badly in need of funds. Could CARE help? I wondered.

Luckily I still had Paula's card so I rang and asked if I could go in to see her. She agreed and I set out on my motor-bike without a clue as to where to find her. I had the address given but Saigon is a very large place! I roamed around for some time asking cyclo drivers which way to go and eventually I arrived at CARE's Office. (I had a map which gave the general area in which to find the address but riding a motorbike and reading a map can be a little difficult. Numbers on buildings very often do not go in sequcnce and roads sometimes change names without any warning.)

Paula was not in a position to help me with funds at that stage but once she knew I was involved in English teaching and lived in Thu Duc she asked if I would be interested in a project CARE was funding for prostitutes at a Rehabilitation Centre in Thu Duc. They needed an English Teacher for smaller groups of these young women, she said. English language learning was the rage at that time and we could help these young women if for no other reason but to help build up their self esteem. She promised to pick me up the next time she was going over, to let me see the set up. Funnily enough the Centre was situated somewhere behind our convent and I had never heard of it.

It was a detention centre run by the Government for prostitutes who had been picked up on the streets by the police. If a young woman could bribe herself out of the situation she would be released, but those who had no money would be taken to the Police Station, held for the night, and the next morning loaded into closed-in trucks and driven out to this detention centre.

Prostitution is illegal in Vietnam but it is estimated that some tens of thousands of girls work in the sex industry. Because of the poverty many Vietnamese families are surviving on the earnings of a prostitute daughter. Among the poor as many as forty people could depend on one sex worker for their bare livelihood. There can be big money involved too - many bars, restaurants, brothels, hotels, taxis, motorbike drivers, pimps, and even police have a vested interest in prostitution.

For a first offence (or, rather, a first conviction) girls were locked up for six months, during which time they were taught the error of their ways and told in no uncertain terms not to return to "that employment" when they were released. The ridiculous part about the whole thing was that the families of these young women had to pay the Centre for food and upkeep during their time there. So, once the girls were able to return home they had no option but to return to the street or brothel to pay back the debt to the family.

CARE was doing wonderful work with these young women, most of whom had no option of employment at that stage. I felt happy to do the little I could by teaching English to those who wanted it. So I began to teach groups of young women and some of the staff once a week, and in time got to know many of them. Whenever an opportunity occurred they would tell me their stories - heart wrenching! They often asked if I would visit them when they went home.

This was easier said than done as we, the outsiders, were never told the girls' real identity or their addresses. If the girl herself gave that information, we had to accept it without letting those in control of the Centre know. They would certainly not have approved. When the Centre was up and running well, NOVIB agreed to fund follow-up and support services for prisoners after release into the community, now that the initial project had been fully equipped and selected staff trained to continue the programmes unaided. International sponsorship had given prestige to the project but as soon as the Centre no longer needed NOVIB's funding, CARE's involvement was stopped, volunteers were no longer wanted, and I was OUT!

The girls' need was now more urgent than ever. I went out once a week, firstly with one or two of our Sisters, to find some of the addresses the girls had given me. We ended up in all sorts of crowded districts and housing complexes but finally were able to locate some of the young women. They and their families were really appreciative of our visits.

The two Sisters who helped me initially had full time jobs at home, one being the full-time Novice Mistress and the other in charge of the Aspirants, so from the outset there was a limit to the amount of time they could give. Paula kindly came up then with the suggestion that an employee of CARE, a Doctor Tri, might like to accompany me each week. This offer was gladly accepted and we worked together each week, following up many of the girls and sometimes assisting them to find work.

One lovely family we visited were very angry at what had happened to their daughter; she was by no means a prostitute but simply happened to be in the wrong place at the wrong time. When police arrived they would collect up any girls in sight, on the merest suspicion, and no-one had a voice or an opportunity to prove their innocence.

Since CARE had run a programme to train the girls in the running of small business projects, we thought it would be good to give them the chance to put their training into practice. We supplied a few of them with "side of the road" stalls, from which they could sell bread, rice, cigarettes or whatever. They tried this out for some time but unfortunately these women had been used to earning big money and could not see the purpose in manning a stall all day for next to nothing. After a few failures, we realized that this was not going to take on. Another reason for failure was that culturally the mother or older woman in the family always ran any business - daughters were there to fetch and carry, and never really learned the intricacies of handling money. They needed a shrewd head for business.

On rethinking our plans we decided that if there was any hope of helping these women they would need to be somewhere removed from the constant demands of their families. In our opinion the greatest need of the women was a sense of self-esteem and personal worth, so we needed to think this through again.

At that particular point I received a message from the woman in charge of the Detention Centre that I was not to try to contact the girls again and if I did she would see that my visa was cancelled. Nothing worthwhile seemed to get any easier!

What I really needed was a full time co-worker, a Vietnamese, who had some knowledge of the conditions of the ordinary people in the street, preferably an older person whom young Vietnamese would naturally look up to. Where would I find a Sister who would be willing to take on such a challenge as this? The Holy Spirit was working away quietly all this time, putting ideas into my head which sometimes I felt more inclined to forget!

Time for a break at the Shelter

I could see the need of a Shelter, a safe place where these girls could come to escape the family pressures and learn to live more normal lives. I discussed this with Paula who was always so positive and encouraging and always ready to share her expertise, but I still had to find the right person to work with me.

An inspiration one evening drove me to contact one of our Sisters who I suddenly knew had all the requirements. When I approached her with this proposal, her first reaction was "But I don't know anything about prostitutes! Give me time to think and pray about it," which we both did! That same evening Sister answered a knock on her door - a young prostitute looking for help! We could not argue with that and so the Sacred Heart Shelter was launched with the blessings of the RNDM Provincial Team.

Through the many contacts Sr. Mary Dominique had, we were able to find a grotty little house which opened on to the street, completely inconspicuous. (This was necessary as the law restricted Religious from working with the people.) We rented this house at a nominal cost.

Our first intake was a handful of girls found on the streets and informed of the Shelter by a former prostitute whom we employed to work in the evenings. Who better would have known the intricacies and the places of 'pick-up' than she?

Sewing lessons commenced on sewing machines purchased and donated by the New Zealand Consulate for which we were very grateful. Another helper/staff member was employed to teach sewing.

Education was a must as most of the girls had missed out on formal education and in many cases they were practically illiterate. We enrolled them in special evening classes and had no problem seeing that they attended. To be educated is a prime desire in Vietnam.

It was essential to start any works on a very small scale without any fanfare so that we would not embarrass the local authorities or show them up in any way. Our funds were very limited at that time so we did not have too many options. As time went on we knew we would have to find sufficient funds if we were going to keep the place running as by that time the assistance from NOVIB was exhausted. We applied to the "Conrad Hilton Fund for Sisters", a bequest set in trust for the use only of Sisters engaged in working with the poor, and that Trust supported our work for the three years to the end of 2005.

As the numbers grew, the house we had was becoming too small. It was dangerous too. There was a small wooden staircase up to a half-floor which I was always afraid would collapse once a few women got up there. We felt we would have to look for something bigger.

Again Sr. Mary Dominique's many friends came to our aid. They found a beautiful house, the type none of us ever dreamed of, and in a cul-de-sac off the noisy main road. It had been built and was owned by a policeman but had never been lived in, in spite of his advertising for clients 'to rent'. He was only too pleased to have someone in it and though the rent was more than for the previous one, it was not outlandish.

The other bonus was that the owner was a policeman. We would not be bothered by police visits to check us out!

How wonderful to have space and be able to expand on three storeys. The girls could hardly believe it when they saw their new home. As the years moved on and the numbers in residence grew we were able to extend our programme with computer skills, hairdressing, sports opportunities e.g. tennis, badminton, swimming and gymnastics in all of which some of them excelled. It did great things in building up their self esteem. Each week a woman doctor came in to teach general health, home and baby care, the dangers of HIV/AIDS etc. For all of this we needed staff. The December 2006 report indicated that the centre had six staff and a full-time cook and house-keeper.

We did not encourage the girls to stay on for too long as this kind of life was too far removed from their normal living in family. Once they felt confident to move on we were happy to let them go, either back to families or into jobs, often in clothing factories. It was up to them then to choose their own life.

We were sorry when after two-and-a-half years we had to go house-hunting again because the owner wanted to use the house himself.

While the Shelter was progressing a side-line from that sprung up without any planning on our part. Single pregnant girls began knocking on the door. It is a great shame for a family in Vietnam to have a daughter become pregnant out of wedlock, so much so, that they will disown them and cast them out on the streets. No-one else will take them in, for fear of the "bad luck" that a disgraced girl would bring on to the household. The only alternative the young woman has is to go to the hospital where, if she has no money, the baby will be aborted. What else could she do?

We could not turn anyone out on to the streets so this sideline of the Shelter sprung up. We did not want these girls following the same programme as the prostitutes, as they were all at different stages of pregnancy. We began to allow them to stay in a little house Sr. M. Dominique called "Home", owned by her family who were in the States. Before we took any girl in, we insisted on her promising to keep the baby once it was born, thc only condition required, because there was much criminal trafficking in children and many unlawful adoptions.

So here was another aspect of our programme growing. We called the little home, Magdala House. Funds to run this came from private donors all over the world as well as local Vietnamese and expatriates. Another staff member was needed, though we expected the girls to look after the house themselves and cook the meals. While they were waiting for the birth of their babies they shared the Skills Programmes with the Shelter, which is not too distant. (Recently Magdala House has been redecorated by the owners and is rented until 2008.)

To date, many girls and their babies have gone through Magdala House. All their expenses are paid by the Centre such as regular doctor check-ups and hospital fees when the baby is born.

We were so lucky, no, blessed is a better word: our progress was more than just luck. When the time came to move the Shelter, a house across the road from Magdala was undergoing renovations and we were able to rent that. Now there are the two houses just across the street from one another, thank God.

Running a programme such as this had its ups and downs but all those involved took it in their stride. They learned to change plans at a moment's notice. (One learns to adapt and allow the works to take their own course while we follow as best we can.) One must bend to a government that can change its policies overnight.

Towards the beginning of 2003 while I was having problems with authorities in Phuoc Long about my visits to the villages, I met a young foreigner who offered me some boxes of 'goods'. His firm was shifting location and they had a lot of stock they could not sell, and wondered if it would be of any use to our projects, either to sell or give away. I knew I would never be able to take this on myself, and Sr. Mary Dominique had more than enough to cope with, so I asked the Sisters who were running the kindergarten schools if they would be interested in the stuff. They were. When it duly arrived at our centre in Thu Duc one evening in three large trucks we were

Some of our first girls with Dominique

One of my classes at Government Centre

amazed to see so many cardboard cartons. They all had to be opened and gone through one by one, but those who took responsibility set to with a vengeance. There were toys and toys and more toys!

Parents bringing their children to school soon became very interested and happily began to buy up toys for their children. All of this was done quite openly. No-one suggested or dreamt there might be anything wrong in this business, or anything that needed to be hidden at the kindergarten. By the end of the week one business woman looked at what was still unsold and offered to take the lot. It was all a wonderful boost for the kindergarten's funds.

That evening about 10.30 p.m. I was woken by voices calling from outside. I reluctantly got up to find one of the Sisters at my door. She informed me that the police had arrived and wanted to see me! I gave her my Passport to take over to show them, another routine check, I thought, and promptly went back to bed!

It was not long before she was back again. The police were still waiting, she said, and getting impatient. "Bother!" I thought, but got up and went over to the door to find out what this fuss was all about. I was confronted with four policemen and four Sisters, the "Welcoming Committee!".

The problem was the 'goods'. Where did they come from? Did I have papers to show they were ours? What was the name of the person who supplied them? Questions! Questions! A lot of useless talk, with one Sister trying to interpret!

Then the police produced an official paper for me to sign. I was not going to be caught like that. No way would I sign unless they could produce the document in English. Sister tried to explain what was written on it but in the end I still could not understand it. I took the risk of signing it in order to get rid of officialdom and protect the Sisters from further trouble.

Before the police left they informed us that they would have to take possession of everything since we had no ownership papers. Did we agree? I was more than pleased to agree just to see the back of them all. I and two other Sisters were told to report to one of the many police stations the following morning.

The next day typical interrogations took place. I'd answered the same questions so many times in so many places I'm sure by now they knew far more about me than I did myself! The toys were duly transferred to police storage. I suspect some people made hay there while the sun shone. The only problem left was with the poor woman who had already paid for the lot: now she was being asked to pay as much again to get her purchases out of custody. Thankfully the first amount she paid was returned to her.

After all that drama, I continued with my work as usual. On 9th May I received in the mail an 'invitation' to attend a meeting at the Immigration Department on visa issues. From the way it was worded I took it for granted that a group of people would be present, and I even rang a few of my friends to see if they would be there.

On the appointed day, 12th May, I arrived at the immigration office at 7.50 a.m. finding, to my surprise, that I was the "privileged one" to be met!

I was escorted to an office upstairs by an official, Mr Nguyen van

Duong, and his secretary, Immigration Department personnel, I thought at the time, the people who had sent the polite invitation. At 8.30 the questioning began, mostly through an interpreter. I think of it now as...

The Saga of the Little Blue Paper

If anyone has ever been through an interrogation procedure they would know how important it is to remember the answers one has given to the questions asked, so that the same answers are given at the following sittings which are sure to follow. The safest way is to stick to the truth!

The usual introduction was to account for who I was, what I was doing in Vietnam and why I was there to start with. As the first sitting progressed I realised that I was not telling them anything they didn't already know.

The questions continued until midday when I was presented with a paper all in Vietnamese about an immigration paper which I had received in 2000 when I returned to the country. This paper was always used when we went to the Police to register our presence in the district.

On the occasion in question, the Police informed us that it was no longer required and consequently was not filled in. It was unfortunate that I had kept it in my passport and so gave them something to use against me. Why had I not presented it?

Eventually I was instructed to go out of the country, preferably to return to New Zealand to get all the right papers! My current Visa would not expire until November 2003. I could not see how I was going to renew a Visa that had not expired.

At one of these meetings my passport was kept. I was told that it would be given back if I wrote down the date on which I would leave the country. I needed also to produce a flight ticket.

On discussing this with people in authority who knew the law, I was told that only one person in Government held the power to send anyone out of the country and it wasn't my local 'friend'. I then solicited the assistance of an overseas lawyer who kindly gave me Trang, one of his office workers, to accompany me to further meetings and this made a marked difference. They had nothing to pin on to me as a good reason why I should not be there.

They kept repeating the phrase, "Your papers are not right" yet they were the papers I had received from Immigration when I came in. How could there be anything wrong with them?

I then got the bright idea and went to my Vietnamese friend who runs a Travel Agency and asked her where I could go out of the country for the day, leave in the morning and return in the afternoon. Cambodia was the nearest so I flew there one morning. On arrival I was asked where I would be staying. "I'll just stay here until the flight returns to Ho Chi Minh City this afternoon!"

They were nonplussed. It took them a while to catch on to that. "Can I wait in transit?" I asked. That seemed to solve any problems, and I did just that. Lunch in the cafeteria and a steaming hot cup of tea set me up for the afternoon. A friend had suggested I take a good book with me. I was pleased I had taken her advice.

On my return to Ho Chi Minh City I received new papers, no different from the ones I had previously had. Now I was all ready for my next visit. Trang, my interpreter, met me at the Immigration Office at 8.30 a.m. We sat in the waiting room watching my 'friend' busying himself backwards and forwards from one office to the other until 9.00 a.m., when he deigned to invite us in.

Have you got your passport?

I rummaged in my bag and took a while to find it before handing it over.

There it is, with all the new papers.

Where did you get these?

From customs at the airport when I returned from Cambodia.

This really floored him and I waited while Trang explained to him that I had been out of the country as he requested.

I thought you'd go back to New Zealand.

He walked out to get some air. When he returned he got down to business and told us I would have to go to the Treasury to pay the 500,000 Vietnamese Dong (approximately $NZ100) fine for not getting a new visa and for doing charitable work without a licence.

This is not logic, I said. The people who issued the renewals should pay the fine, not me. I had to pay to get it done.

You have to get it done at Immigration. Not through a travel agent.

Trang came in then with the query, "How about all the people offering visas to anyone who wants them and sometimes they can be issued in two days. Just go along the street outside here and you will see them everywhere."

I don't know what he replied to that, it was all in Vietnamese.

I will keep your passport until next week to check up on the people who issued it and the travel agency.

Why can't you take a copy of it? I was not letting him get away with anything.

With that he gave me the copy I had provided him with in the beginning.

This one doesn't have the current visa in it.

He handed me a copy of the new visa just to keep me quiet.

You need to go out to New Zealand as soon as possible to get a new visa and then everything will be straight.

I didn't say what I was thinking -**"Much cheaper to get a new one here."**

With that we bade him goodbye, with the assurance that I would return with the receipt from the Treasury after I paid the fee.

This fuss all seemed to come to an end once I had reported the whole scenario to a high Vietnamese Official who followed it up; he went to Immigration to meet with the Officer who had interviewed me on each occasion. On asking to see him, he was informed that no-one by that name worked there - at that time his name was clearly written on the front of his uniform! After that I had no more trouble and continued to do what I could until my current Visa would expire on 10 November 2003.

Chapter 12

COUNTDOWN

Six months remained before my current visa ran out so it was with a heavy heart I set to work to put everything into order so that the projects could continue once I was gone. This meant I had to spend much time with the bank and the solicitor's office making sure everything was clear and workable.

I continued my monthly visits to the villages though access was becoming markedly more difficult. While the Province People's Commmittee wanted me to continue the work of supplying better housing and wells in one particular village there were others who were opposed to this, and this made my life difficult.

For example, my visits to the leper patients were now interrupted by the local police who would appear from nowhere and request my presence at the Police Station a few kilometres from the village. They would not accept my suggestion that I would call in on the way out when I had finished what I was doing. Immediate presence was insisted upon. Off we went for another two hours questioning to further establish my identity and my real purpose for being there.

At one of these police meetings there was an older man present. When he learnt that I had worked in Phuoc Long in and before 1975 he was adamant that I should not be helping anyone now and that I should be sent packing! All the time I was anxious about the amount

Bella, one of the monkeys we looked after while in Ho Chi Minh City

of time being wasted as my work was not finished in the village and there was still a two hour drive back to Saigon ahead of us. One particular difficulty was ensuring that the leper patients still received the supplements their diets required. We overcame this by sending one of our local helpers on his motorbike to transport the necessary supplies.

My last visit to all the villages before I left was on the back of my trusty motorbike, a hair raising experience over walking tracks through the forest, over streams and up hills hanging on by the skin of my teeth.

I also needed to visit the Shelter in Saigon to meet with the Sisters and ensure that the girls were provided for. This took much travel time through the city's chaotic traffic on my faithful motorbike which I am sure knew the routes off by heart!

As the time for my departure drew closer, I had to see to all the packing up, sorting out final details about the future life of the different projects and, above all, farewelling the many wonderful friends who had supported me in Vietnam. It was precisely because they had been so supportive and caring that I knew I would miss them so much.

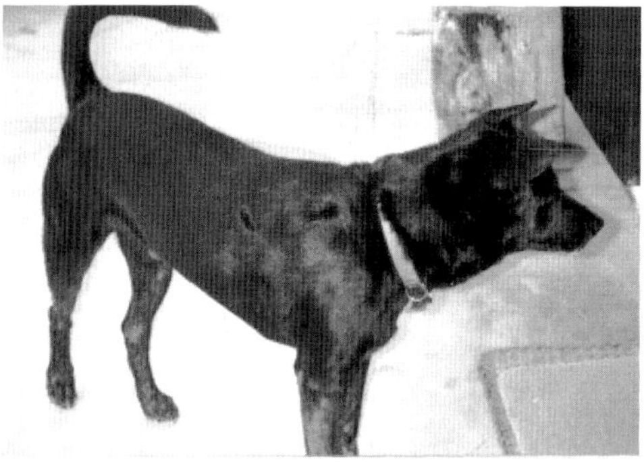

Buttons and Shadow, these two dogs we rescued from the markets.

Bobby had only one hand

The twelve years that had elapsed since my return to Vietnam had gone by all too quickly. Much had happened in the country in those years. In particular, the arrival of many NGOs (non-government organizations) to work in so many needy areas was helping to lift education standards and improve the health of thousands of Vietnamese. But over and above the work of the NGOs was the wonderful faith of the Vietnamese themselves. Whether Buddhist, Christian or traditional, the Vietnamese people have a wonderful inner strength that sustains them in the often difficult situations in which they find themselves, enabling them to move forward toward a better future.

While economic growth has improved the general living standards of many, there are still many others struggling to eke out a daily existence. However, I firmly believe that all the peoples of this wonderful land are truly resilient and their strong sense of humour, their willingness to work and to struggle against adversity means they are on the road to freedom.

So as the date of departure approached I thanked God for all that had been, I prepared to say "Yes" to all that will be, in the sure knowledge that there is a loving God whose light will overcome the darkness. I was farewelling a country and a people who had given me so much more than I could ever give.

Appendix A

Sacred Heart Shelter

Saigon - Vietnam

2006 Summary Of Progress

Since 1998 Sacred Heart Shelter has been established to cater for vulnerable young women - prostitutes - in and around the Saigon area as well as districts further afield where young women have come from, mostly by word of mouth, to find help to escape the clutches of the greedy who exploit them. Here they have been able to build up their self esteem again and prepare to live a normal healthy life.

Much has changed within the country during these past seven years. Those in the city have become more affluent while the poor and vulnerable have been used, often unsuspectingly to help fill the pockets of those more wily.

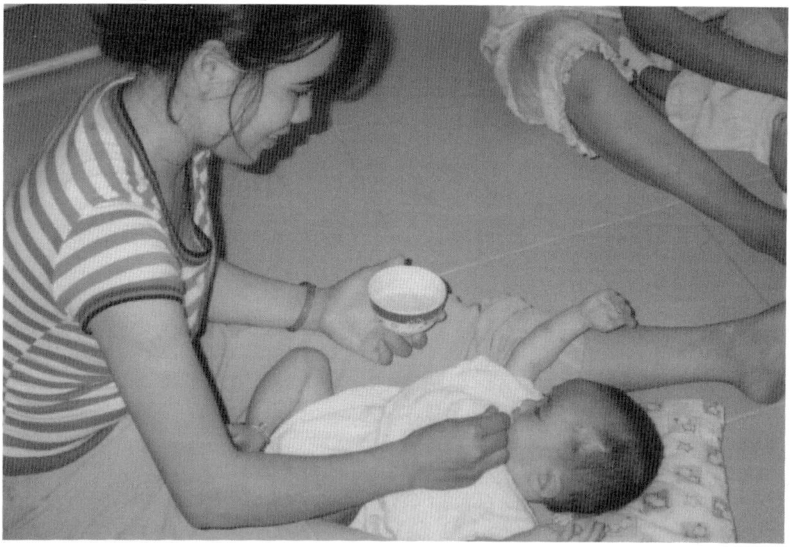

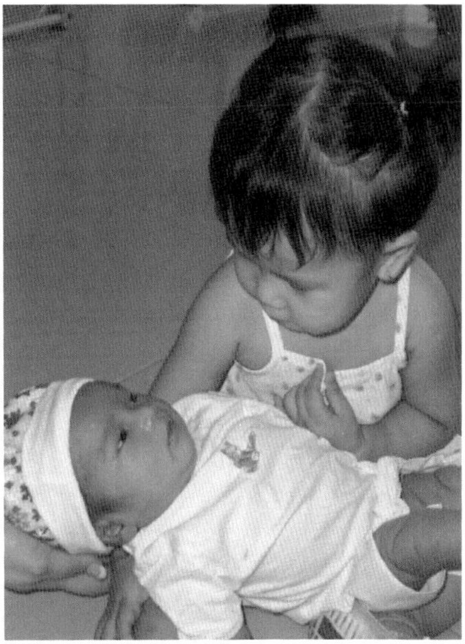

Money has become the 'be all' and 'end all' for so many and others are exploited to attain this end. Drugs and alcohol are readily available and the unsuspecting are easy prey.

Poverty in the rural areas forces many young women into the city to find some work that may give them a little money that they can send home to help the family. They do not experience a very high level of education so that it becomes harder for these girls to find any jobs.

Factories abound and use these girls for cheap labour if they are lucky enough to produce the identity card required. The lack of one of these could land them up in prison so they often have to borrow their brother's or sister's card and hope they won't be detected.

In order to get started six young people, consisting of three couples, may rent a small room barely large enough for two. If there are more single girls one will take it on herself to teach the others how to 'make up' and the use of a cell phone. Once they have passed the 'test' they can then contact a nearby hotel and become 'private prostitutes' close to home without the danger of being on the streets.

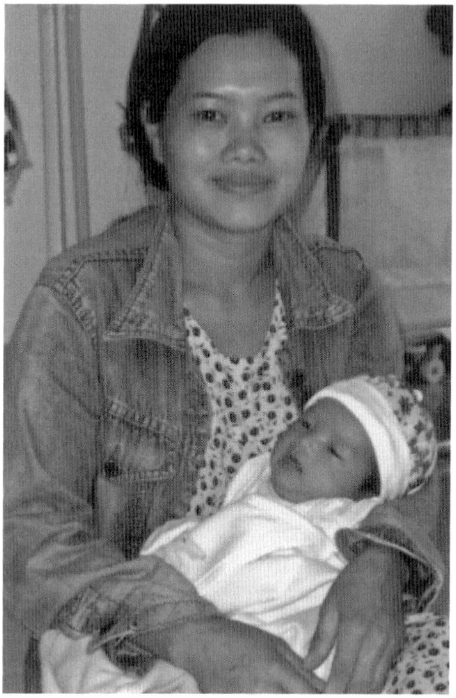 

Every day the hospitals are visited by many of these young women requesting abortions. If the foetus is already four or five months a concerned nurse will give them the address and telephone number of Sacred Heart Shelter where they will be welcomed.

In 2006, 73 young women have been able to use the facilities we offer. They have had time to prepare for the birth of their babies, learn skills such as sewing, hairdressing, child care, cooking, education at evening classes and in general regain their self esteem. All this is made available with the help of an experienced staff of five persons full time and two part time.

The Shelter originally founded to assist prostitutes is now catering for more and more single mothers. At present we have 11 single mothers and 11 babies with one small child who attends school, plus five pregnant girls. To date 49 mothers have returned to their families over the years with beautiful healthy babies. Four prostitutes have also gone home to begin a new life.

The Visitation House, our newly established second house, has been set up to cater for the overflow. Here there are nine pregnant girls ranging from three to eight months pregnant. Here the same courses are taught by the staff spreading out to cover all.

Time for fun, outings and relaxation is also available and badminton for those still agile enough, swimming in the public swimming pool, while TV, video and radio help to keep them up with the daily happenings around the world - much bigger than their own.

All that you have read here has been made possible purely by the donations of so many of our friends. We thank each of you and remember you in our daily prayers.

Sr. Sheila O'Toole,
Sisters of the Missions,
23 Victoria Avenue,
Morrinsville,
New Zealand

Sr. Dominic Hao,
Sisters of the Missions,
40 Ben Cat - P7,
Tan Binh,
TP Ho Chi Minh City,
Vietnam

Appendix B

Chronology Of Events

1887 Vietnam becomes part of French Indo-China

1924 Mission Sisters establish a mission in (North) Vietnam

1928 Sister Gwen Mary McCarthy (Sister Mary Floride) in Vietnam 1928-1954 and 1958-1969

1939-45 World War II - Vietnam occupied by Japanese forces

1945 Vietnam declares its independence but French rule continues

1954 France defeated by Vietnamese Communist forces under Ho Chi Minh. Under the Geneva Accords of 1954, Vietnam was divided into the Communist North and anti-Communist South

1954 Mission Sisters leave North Vietnam and establish themselves in South Vietnam

1954 US economic and military aid to South Vietnam grew through the 1960s in an attempt to support the South Vietnamese Government

1969 Sheila O'Toole (then known as Sister Mary Laurence) goes to South Vietnam

1973 A cease-fire agreement led to the withdrawal of US forces

1974 Dorothy Dickson arrives in Vietnam

1975 North Vietnamese forces overran the South reuniting the country under Communist rule

1975 Saigon renamed as Ho Chi Minh City

1975 Sheila O'Toole and Dorothy Dickson leave Vietnam

1986 Vietnamese Government introduces some free-market reforms

1986 Sheila O'Toole receives the Queen's Service Order

1992 Sheila O'Toole goes to Vietnam with a VSA team and continues to work with the underprivileged there

2003 Sheila O'Toole returns to New Zealand and is awarded a Companion of the New Zealand Order of Merit

Appendix C

VIETNAM AFTER 1975